Mac OS® X
v.10.3 Panther™

TOP 100
Simplified®

Tips & Tricks

by Mark L. Chambers and Erick Tejkowski

From
maranGraphics®

&

Ⓦ
Wiley Publishing, Inc.

Visual™

Mac OS® X v.10.3 Panther™:

Top 100 Simplified® Tips & Tricks

Published by
Wiley Publishing, Inc.
111 River Street
Hoboken, NJ 07030-5774

Published simultaneously in Canada

Copyright © 2004 by Wiley Publishing, Inc.,
Indianapolis, Indiana

Certain designs, text, and illustrations Copyright
© 1992-2004 maranGraphics, Inc., used with
maranGraphics's permission.

maranGraphics, Inc.
5755 Coopers Avenue
Mississauga, Ontario, Canada
L4Z 1R9

Library of Congress Control Number: Available
from Publisher
ISBN: 0-7645-4395-4
Manufactured in the United States of America
10 9 8 7 6 5 4 3 2 1

1K/RS/QR/QU/IN

Trademark Acknowledgments

Important Numbers

For U.S. corporate orders, please call maranGraphics at
(800)469-6616 or fax (905)890-9434.

For general information on our other products and
services or to obtain technical support please contact
our Customer Care Department within the United
States at (800)762-2974, outside the United States
at (317)572-3993 or fax (317)572-4002.

Wiley Publishing, Inc.

U.S. Corporate Sales	**U.S. Trade Sales**
Contact maranGraphics at (800) 469-6616 or fax (905) 890-9434.	Contact Wiley at (800) 762-2974 or fax (317) 572-4002.

CREDITS

Project Editor:
Dana Rhodes Lesh

Acquisitions Editor:
Jody Lefevere

Product Development Manager:
Lindsay Sandman

Copy Editor:
Dana Rhodes Lesh

Technical Editor:
Debbie Gates

Editorial Manager:
Robyn Burnett

Editorial Assistant:
Adrienne Porter

Manufacturing:
Allan Conley
Linda Cook
Paul Gilchrist
Jennifer Guynn

Illustrators:
Ronda David-Burroughs
David E. Gregory

Book Design:
maranGraphics, Inc.

Production Coordinator:
Maridee Ennis

Layout:
Beth Brooks
LeAndra Hosier
Kristin McMullan

Screen Artists:
Jill A. Proll
Lynsey Osborn

Proofreaders/Quality Control:
John Greenough
Susan Moritz

Indexer:
Ty Koontz

Vice President and Executive Group Publisher:
Richard Swadley

Vice President and Publisher:
Barry Pruett

Director of Composition Services:
Debbie Stailey

ABOUT THE AUTHORS

Mark L. Chambers has been an author, computer consultant, programmer, and hardware technician for more than 20 years. With a degree in journalism and creative writing from Louisiana State University, Mark took the logical career choice and started programming computers. However, after five years as a COBOL programmer for a hospital system, he became the documentation manager for Datastorm Technologies, a well-known communications software developer. Somewhere in between organizing and writing software manuals, Mark began writing computer books; his first book, *Running a Perfect BBS,* was published in 1994. Along with writing several books a year, Mark has recently branched out into Web-based education, designing and teaching a number of online classes — called *WebClinics* — for Hewlett-Packard.

Mark's list of books includes *Mac OS X All-in-One Desk Reference For Dummies, Microsoft Office v. X Power User's Guide, Teach Yourself the iMac VISUALLY, Building a PC For Dummies, Scanners For Dummies,* and *CD and DVD Recording For Dummies.* Mark welcomes all comments and questions about his books; you can reach him at mark@mlcbooks.com or visit MLC Books Online, his Web site, at www.mlcbooks.com.

Erick Tejkowski is an author and programmer. In addition to writing books on Mac OS X Jaguar, Cocoa programming, and REALbasic, he is a regular contributor to periodicals such as *MacTech, MacWorld,* and *MacAddict.* Erick also serves on the editorial board of *REALbasic Developer* magazine. He lives near St. Louis, Missouri, with his wife, Lisa, and children, Mercedes and Leopold.

maranGraphics is a family-run business
located near Toronto, Canada.

At **maranGraphics**, we believe
in producing great computer
books — one book at a time.

Each maranGraphics book uses
the award-winning communication
process that we have been
developing over the last 28 years.
Using this process, we organize
screenshots and text in a way
that makes it easy for you to
learn new concepts and tasks.

We spend hours deciding the
best way to perform each task,
so you don't have to! Our clear,
easy-to-follow screenshots and
instructions walk you through
each task from beginning to end.

We want to thank you for
purchasing what we feel are
the best computer books money
can buy. We hope you enjoy using
this book as much as we enjoyed
creating it!

Sincerely,

The Maran Family

Please visit us on the Web at
www.maran.com

HOW TO USE THIS BOOK

Mac OS® X v.10.3 Panther: Top 100 Simplified® Tips & Tricks includes the 100 most interesting and useful tasks that you can perform in Mac OS X Panther. This book reveals cool secrets and time-saving tricks guaranteed to make you more productive.

Who is this book for?

Are you a visual learner who already knows the basics of Mac OS X Panther but would like to take your Panther experience to the next level? Then this is the book for you.

Conventions in This Book

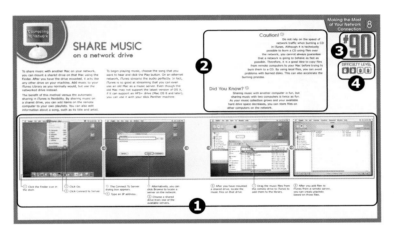

❶ Steps

This book walks you through each task using a step-by-step approach. Lines and "lassos" connect the screenshots to the step-by-step instructions to show you exactly how to perform each task.

❷ Tips

Fun and practical tips answer questions that you have always wondered about. Plus, learn to do things in Mac OS X Panther that you never thought were possible!

❸ Task Numbers

The task numbers, ranging from 1 to 100, indicate which self-contained lesson you are currently working on.

❹ Difficulty Levels

For quick reference, symbols mark the difficulty level of each task.

 Demonstrates a new spin on a common task

 Introduces a new skill or a new task

 Combines multiple skills requiring in-depth knowledge

 Requires extensive skill and may involve other technologies

TABLE OF CONTENTS

① Customizing Your Desktop

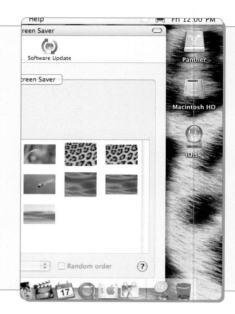

Task #1   Add Your Own Desktop Background 4

#2   Change Desktops Automatically 6

#3   Change Menu Colors 7

#4   Switch Video Resolutions 8

#5   Use Font Smoothing..9

#6   Configure the Clock 10

#7   Select an Alert Sound 12

#8   Customize Your Mouse 14

#9   Display or hide Desktop Icons 15

#10   Configure Visual and Audio Aids 16

#11   Customize the Finder..18

② Managing Files and Folders

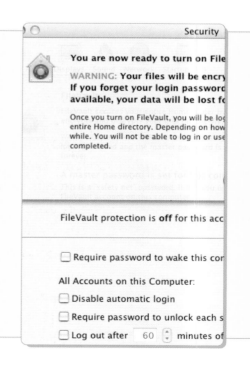

Task #12   Accelerate File Access with Panther's New Places Sidebar 22

#13   Use Spring-Loaded Folders to Reduce Clutter.............................24

#14   Access Contexual Menu Commands...25

#15   Leverage Keyboard Shortcuts to Speed up Work 26

#16   Find Files in a Flash 28

#17   Use Color Labels..29

#18   Access File Information with Get Info 30

#19   Open a File without Using the Default Application......................31

#20   Copy Files Four Different Ways..32

#21   Create an Alias 34

#22   Customize Icons of Files and Folders 36

#23   Navigate Panther's New Open and Save Dialog Boxes 37

#24   Protect Files from Prying Eyes 38

3 Using Panther More Efficiently

Task #25   Add and Delete Dock Icons 42

#26   Add Web Sites to the Dock 43

#27   Customize the Finder Toolbar 44

#28   Relocate and Resize the Dock 45

#29   Configure Exposé 46

#30   Launch Recent Items 47

#31   Put Your Mac to Sleep..48

#32   Switch Between Users 49

#33   Start or Shut Down Your Mac Automatically 50

#34   Hide and Display the Finder Toolbar 51

#35   Use the Go Menu 52

#36   Save Time with Keyboard Shortcuts 53

#37   Work Automatically with CD and DVD Discs 54

#38   Use Mac OS X Services 55

#39   View Files with Preview 56

4 Expanding Your Mac's Horizons

Task #40   Connect to Other Devices with iSync 60

#41   Use Stickies on Your Desktop 61

#42   Access UNIX With Terminal 62

#43   Delete Your Trash Securely 63

#44   Protect Your Privacy with FileVault 64

#45   Start Applications Automatically When You Log In.......65

#46   Activate Voice Commands 66

#47   Save Documents as PDF Files 67

#48   Run Multiple Versions of Mac OS 68

#49   Configure Your Personal Address Book Card 69

#50   Add a New Font 70

#51   Take Screenshots with Grab 71

#52   Add a New Event in iCal 72

#53   Editing Text Files with TextEdit 74

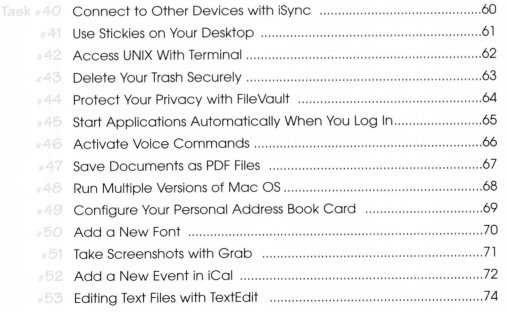

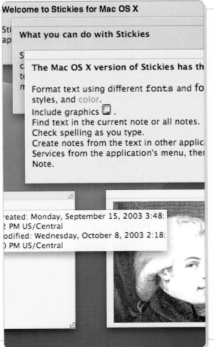

TABLE OF CONTENTS

5 Working with Multimedia and the Digital Hub

Task #54 Get Photos, Movies, and Music onto Your Mac 78

#55 Convert Audio with iTunes 80

#56 Burn DVDs with iDVD 81

#57 Burn CDs and DVDs with iTunes 82

#58 Use iTunes Audio in iMovie 84

#59 Use iPhoto Images in iMovie.......................86

#60 Fade iMovie Audio In and Out 88

#61 Add or Remove the Ken Burns Effect 90

#62 Export iMovies for Use in the Hub.......................92

#63 Export iPhoto Images 94

#64 Use iTunes to Crop and Split Files.......................96

6 Troubleshooting Problems and Seeking Help

Task #65 Force a Program to Quit 100

#66 Use Mac OS X Help 101

#67 Fix Hard Drive Problems with the Disk Utility 102

#68 Find out Hardware and Software Information with the System Profiler 104

#69 Monitor Your Mac's Performance 105

#70 Search the AppleCare Knowledge Base 106

#71 Update Mac OS X 107

#72 Boot from a CD-ROM 108

#73 Uninstall Applications the Correct Way 109

#74 Fix Problems with User Accounts 110

#75 Rebuild the Classic Mode Desktop 112

7 Taking Advantage of the Internet

Task #76 Organize Your Web Surfing with Tabs 116

#77 View and Bookmark Documents In Safari 118

#78 Save Web Pages on Your Hard Drive 119

#79 Stop Pop-Up Ads from Appearing in Your Browser 120

#80 Eliminate Spam with Mail 121

#81 Manage Threaded E-Mail..122

#82 Set Up a Web Server 123

#83 Visit Web Sites of People in Your Address Book 124

#84 Use Rendezvous to Surf Local Web Sites 125

#85 Save Internet Content for Later Use 126

#86 Use Sherlock to Find Information and Perform Tasks................128

#87 Channel the Power of the Address Book in Mail......................130

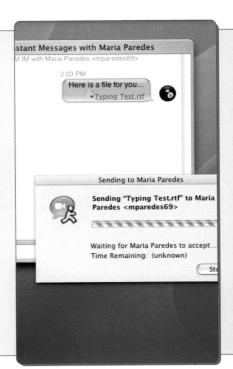

8 Making the Most of Your Network Connection

Task #88 Share Music over Your Network with iTunes 134

#89 Audio and Video Conferencing with iChat 135

#90 Share Music on a Network Drive 136

#91 Download Files with FTP 138

#92 Remotely Control Other Computers on Your Network 140

#93 Protect Your Computer with a Firewall 142

#94 Share Files with Windows Computers 143

#95 Share Printers with Other Computers 144

#96 Unfreeze a Frozen Mac over the Network 146

#97 Share Files with iChat 148

#98 Use iChat Keyboard Shortcuts 150

#99 Fax Files from Any Application 151

#100 Share an iPod on a Network 152

CHAPTER 1

Customizing Your Desktop

Any Panther power user will tell you that customizing your Mac OS X desktop is an important key to improved productivity — after all, if you know where your tools are and you have arranged things to your satisfaction, you are going to work faster and with less effort! To be honest, I find that even a so-called "minor" change to the desktop, such as a new background picture, can help me maintain focus (and keep smiling) after a long day of work.

In fact, many readers whom I have met over the years seem to think that you have to be a software developer, Hollywood video editor, or professional musician to "warrant" customizing the way Panther looks; this is *definitely* not true. Even if you use your Mac only an hour or so

every day, you will enjoy your time behind the keyboard far more if your desktop is arranged to your preferences. Consider the effect of changing just your video resolution: With only two or three mouse clicks, you immediately have more area available to create and edit your documents.

Most of the tips in this chapter cover changes to the look of your desktop, which makes sense: Because the Macintosh has used a graphical operating system from the very beginning, Mac OS X is a visual feast for the eyes. You will learn the steps you should take to configure your desktop clock and the Finder window toolbar, as well as features for those with reduced vision.

TOP 100

#1   Add your own desktop background. . . 4

#2   Change desktops automatically 6

#3   Change menu colors 7

#4   Switch video resolutions 8

#5   Use font smoothing 9

#6   Configure the clock 10

#7   Select an alert sound 12

#8   Customize your mouse 14

#9   Display or hide desktop icons 15

#10   Configure visual and audio aids 16

#11   Customize the Finder 18

Add your own
DESKTOP
BACKGROUND

Apple ships a number of attractive background images with Mac OS X, including abstract artwork and nature photos, but I have yet to meet a computer owner who does not prefer using a favorite image for a desktop background. In fact, if you have created a library of digital photographs using iPhoto, Panther makes it easy to select an image from your library for use as a desktop background. Alternatively, you can opt for a solid color background instead of an image.

With the selection of images available for downloading from the Web, it is no wonder that you can browse through your hard drive for desktop pictures in both Mac OS X and Windows XP. Within Mac OS X, you can use the Desktop & Screen Saver pane in System Preferences to choose an image for your desktop background.

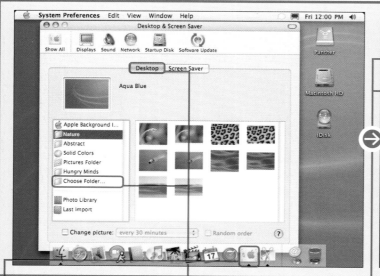

① Click the System Preferences icon in the dock.

○ The System Preferences dialog box appears.

② Click the Desktop & Screen Saver icon.

○ The Desktop & Screen Saver pane appears.

③ Click Desktop to select a picture.

④ Click Choose Folder.

○ A File Open dialog box opens.

⑤ Click the hard drive that holds the image you want to use.

⑥ Double-click the folder that holds the image that you want.

○ If the image is stored in a subfolder, double-click it to select it.

⑦ Click Choose to display the pictures in the selected folder.

DIFFICULTY LEVEL

Did You Know? ※

Although any JPEG or TIFF format image can be used as a background picture, images of 640 x 480 or larger will look the best using the Fill Screen option. If the image that you want to use is smaller than 640 x 480, click the Fill Screen drop-down list box on the Desktop & Screen Saver pane and click Tile, which covers your desktop with multiple copies of the image.

Did You Know? ※

If you would like to use an image that you have stored in your Pictures folder, click Pictures Folder on the Desktop & Screen Saver pane. Panther immediately displays thumbnails of any images that you have saved to the folder. Because many applications use your Pictures folder as a default location for saving image files, this "shortcut" can save you time.

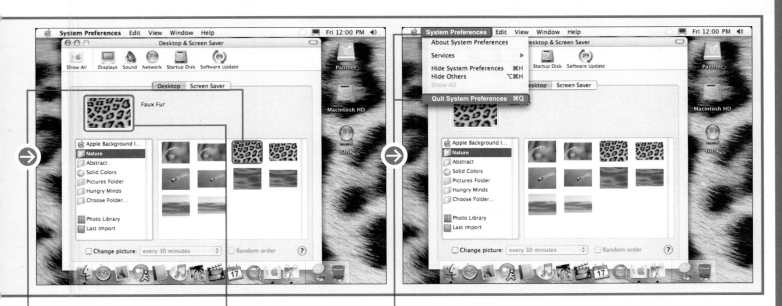

⑧ Click the picture that you want to use.

○ The selected image appears in the preview well at the top of the dialog box.

⑨ Click System Preferences.

⑩ Click Quit System Preferences.

○ Mac OS X saves your changes and displays your new desktop background.

CHANGE DESKTOPS
automatically

Instead of manually changing your Mac OS X desktop background, you can *automatically* switch to a new desktop after a specified amount of time — without ever clicking a single control! You can even choose to rotate the display of images from a selected folder, or Panther can surprise you and choose one at random.

You set up this feature using the Desktop & Screen Saver pane in System Preferences.

Expect a certain amount of disk activity and a pause of a few seconds when Panther is busy changing

your background. If you find this annoying, you can always configure Panther to disable automatic background changes altogether.

Note that two other options are included for triggering a desktop background change: You can choose to switch backgrounds when you are logging in, which also works if you are using fast user switching, and Panther can load a new background each time your Mac wakes from sleep mode.

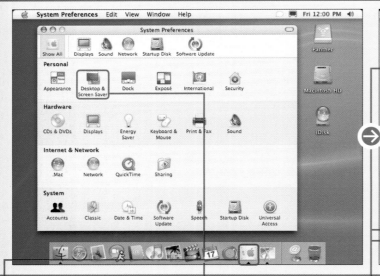

① Click the System Preferences icon in the dock.

○ The System Preferences dialog box appears.

② Click the Desktop & Screen Saver icon.

○ The Desktop & Screen Saver pane appears.

③ Click Desktop.

④ Click Change Picture (☐ changes to ☑).

○ Mac OS X enables the delay and random controls.

⑤ Click the delay drop-down list box and select the time you want the background to change.

○ If you want Mac OS X to randomly select a background from the specified folder, click Random Order (☐ changes to ☑).

⑥ Click System Preferences ➪ Quit System Preferences.

Change MENU COLORS

#3

DIFFICULTY LEVEL

There are two colorful decisions that you have to make when customizing the look of your Panther desktop: You can set the Appearance color, which determines the coloring used in controls such as drop-down list boxes and buttons, and the Highlight color, which governs the color used when you highlight text in applications such as Word and Safari.

Besides the aesthetic improvement to your desktop, customizing these colors may help some visually impaired Mac users recognize highlighted text and application or operating system controls more easily than they would with the default colors.

If you have switched to Panther's reversed White on Black text option — using the settings in the Universal Access pane in System Preferences — these menu colors will naturally be disabled. The White on Black option is provided for those Mac users who have connected assistive devices, or Mac users who have trouble seeing the standard black on a white screen.

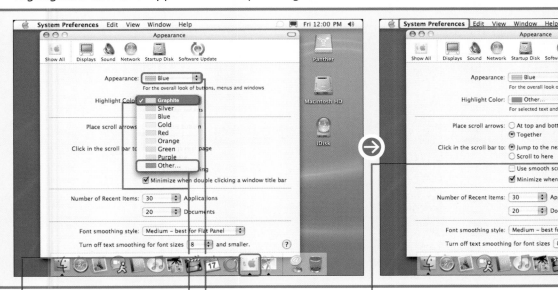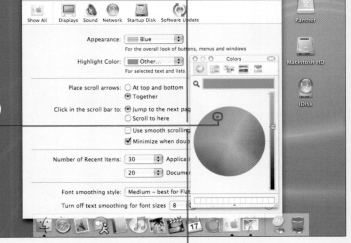

① Click the System Preferences icon in the dock.

② Click the Appearance icon.

○ The Appearance pane of the System Preferences dialog box appears.

③ Click the Appearance drop-down list box and select Blue or Graphite.

○ You can click the Highlight Color drop-down list box and choose a color.

④ To specify your own highlight color, click Other.

○ The Colors palette appears, in which you can click any color displayed in the wheel.

⑤ Click System Preferences.

⑥ Click Quit System Preferences.

Switch
VIDEO RESOLUTIONS

 # #4

Mac OS X can use a number of different video resolutions, depending on the combination of the graphics card and monitor that you are using. You may want to switch to a higher resolution when you need to work on a large-format document — such as a super-sized digital photograph or a detailed PowerPoint slide. Many Mac users prefer a lower video resolution for playing games and general readability.

Did You Know? ☀

If you enable the Show Displays in Menu Bar check box in the Displays pane of the System Preferences dialog box, you can also click the Monitor icon in the menu bar at the top of the Mac OS X desktop; a menu appears with the most common video resolutions, and you can switch immediately to another resolution by clicking the resolution that you want. If you need to make a change to the display settings in System Preferences, you can also open the Displays pane from this menu.

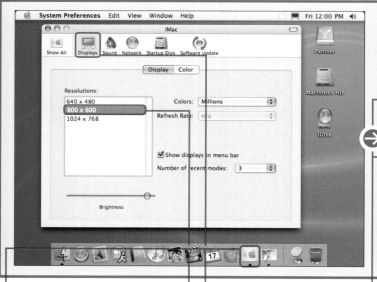

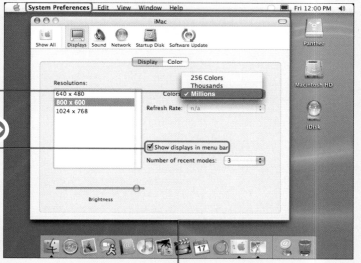

① Click the System Preferences icon in the dock.

○ The System Preferences dialog box appears.

② Click the Displays icon.

○ The Displays pane appears.

③ Click the resolution that you want.

④ Click the Colors drop-down list box and choose the highest number of colors available.

⑤ Click Show Displays in Menu Bar to enable the check box (☐ changes to ☑).

Note: This enables you to choose a resolution from the Mac OS X desktop menu bar.

⑥ Click System Preferences.

⑦ Click Quit System Preferences.

Use FONT SMOOTHING

 #5

DIFFICULTY LEVEL

Font smoothing is a feature designed to improve the appearance and readability of the text displayed on your monitor — whether that text is displayed within an application or on the Panther desktop. Mac OS X can reduce the jagged edges surrounding the text, making it look sharper.

You can specify the maximum size for font smoothing, as well as choose the smoothing style to best fit the type of monitor that you are using (and your eyesight!).

Did You Know? ☀

You cannot turn off font smoothing altogether, but you can reduce the effects to as little as possible. This may be a good idea if you are working with an older monitor, or you would rather not spend the processing time. (The display speed of your Mac slows down slightly if you use font smoothing.) Set the smoothing style to Light and turn off smoothing for font sizes 12 and smaller.

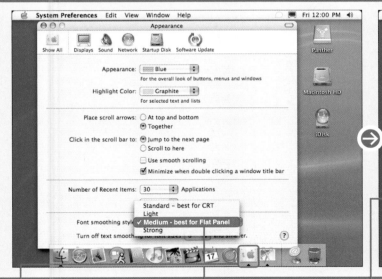

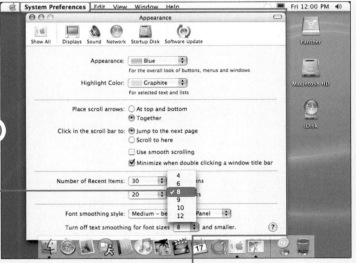

① Click the System Preferences icon in the dock.

○ The System Preferences dialog box appears.

② Click the Appearance icon.

○ The Appearance pane appears.

③ Click the Font Smoothing Style drop-down list box and choose the type of smoothing that you prefer.

Note: Standard is best for traditional monitors, whereas Medium is best for flat-panel LCD displays.

④ Click the Turn Off Text Smoothing drop-down list box and choose the maximum font size to be smoothed.

⑤ Click System Preferences.

⑥ Click Quit System Preferences.

CONFIGURE
the clock

How could something as simple as a clock be so important? Try going without the correct time for an entire day! Apple recognizes the value of a good timepiece, and this is reflected in Mac OS X — where you can easily customize the appearance, behavior, and location of the desktop clock in the Date & Time pane of System Preferences.

Panther provides a time announcement feature that I highly recommend. Enable the Announce the Time check box and specify the time period that you want; I find that this automated announcement helps me keep track of passing time while I work.

If you are traveling with your Mac notebook, you will probably need to change the time zone often. Panther makes this easy: Just select the closest city to your current location in the Time Zone pane, which is also a part of the Date & Time pane.

Panther enables you to switch to an international format for your clock's date and time — but because all international formats are handled from the International pane in System Preferences, you will find a convenient Open International button to take you to the proper settings.

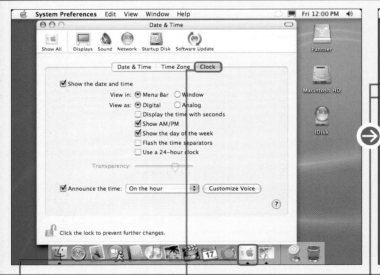

① Click the System Preferences icon in the dock.

○ The System Preferences dialog box appears.

② Click the Date & Time icon.

○ The Date & Time pane appears.

③ Click Clock.

④ Click Show the Date and Time to enable the check box (☐ changes to ☑).

⑤ Click either the Menu Bar or Window option to specify where the clock should appear (○ changes to ◉).

Note: If you click Window, you can click and drag the clock window to any spot on your desktop.

Did You Know? ☀

If your Mac has an Internet connection, you can configure Panther's clock to automatically update the time from an Internet time server. To do so, in the Date & Time pane, click the Set Date & Time Automatically check box to enable it. You can then click the check box's drop-down list box to select an Apple Internet time server.

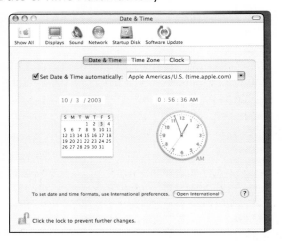

DIFFICULTY LEVEL

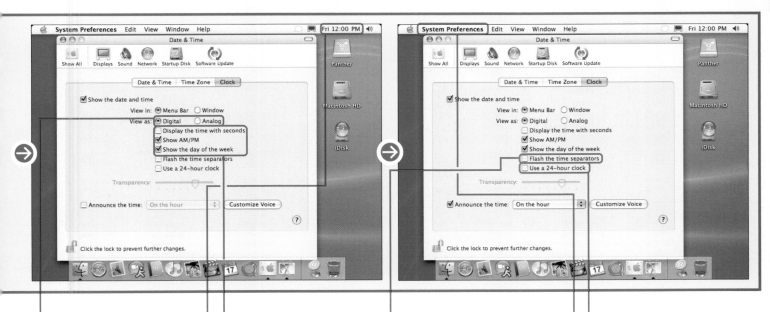

(6) Click either the Digital or Analog option to determine the appearance of the clock (○ changes to ◉).

(7) Click the Display the Time with Seconds, Show AM/PM, and Show the Day of the Week check boxes to customize the digital clock display (☐ changes to ☑).

○ The clock is immediately updated to show your changes.

○ If you are using a digital clock, you can click Flash the Time Separators to indicate the seconds (☐ changes to ☑).

○ If you are using a digital clock, you can click Use a 24-Hour Clock to display the time in the 24-hour military fashion (☐ changes to ☑).

(8) Click System Preferences.

(9) Click Quit System Preferences.

Select an
ALERT SOUND

With the settings on the Sound pane in System Preferences, the Mac OS X desktop can keep you abreast of important events even if you are across the room by providing you with an alert sound — or you can decide to eliminate alert sounds entirely for quiet computing.

By default, Panther plays alert sounds at many points: if an application displays a message or warning dialog box, for example, or when you click certain controls within some application windows and

system dialog boxes. You can turn some of these sounds off, and it is easy to control the overall system volume — or mute all sound entirely.

You can control the volume levels of all sound played by your Macintosh, including the audio produced by games and other applications, by using the Sound pane in System Preferences. Adjusting the Output Volume setting is equivalent to pressing the Volume Up or Volume Down keys on your keyboard.

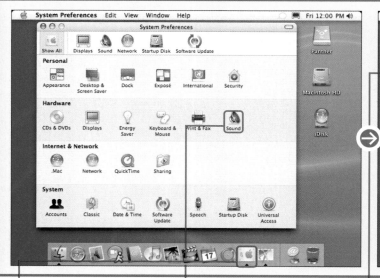

① Click the System Preferences icon in the dock.

O The System Preferences dialog box appears.

② Click the Sound icon.

O The Sound pane appears.

③ Click Sound Effects.

④ Click an alert sound effect in the list.

O Panther plays the sound effect so that you can decide if you like it.

⑤ Click the Alert Volume slider and drag it to the spot that you want.

Note: This volume level is dependent on the overall Output volume; if you raise or lower the Output volume, the Alert volume also changes.

#7

DIFFICULTY LEVEL

Did You Know? ☀

Checking the Mute check box in the Sound pane is handy when you want to immediately turn off all sound on your computer — for example, on your notebook Mac when you are on the road. Using this check box is equivalent to pressing the Mute key on your keyboard.

Customize It! ☀

If your keyboard does not have volume keys — or if you often need to rapidly change the volume on your system — click the Show Volume in Menu Bar check box in the Sound pane to enable it. You can click and drag using your mouse to adjust the Volume control at the far right of the Finder menu, and the Volume icon itself changes to indicate the relative volume setting.

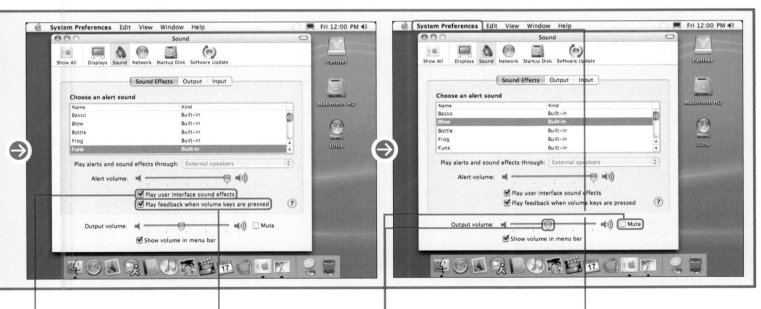

⑥ Click Play User Interface Sound Effects to enable (or disable) the sound effects that accompany changes to controls and menu selections (☐ changes to ☑).

⑦ Click Play Feedback When Volume Keys Are Pressed to enable (or disable) the sound effects played when you press the Volume Up and Volume Down keys on your keyboard (☐ changes to ☑).

⑧ Click the Output Volume slider and drag it to the spot that you want.

⑨ To mute all sound on your Macintosh, click Mute to enable the check box (☐ changes to ☑).

⑩ Click System Preferences.

⑪ Click Quit System Preferences.

○ Your new alert sound settings are saved.

CUSTOMIZE
your mouse

In the world of the graphical user interface — or GUI, as it is commonly called — the mouse pointer is king; therefore, Panther enables you to fine-tune your mouse's behavior to match your preferences.

Even if you have been using Mac OS X for months now, you may find yourself returning to the Keyboard & Mouse pane in System Preferences when you buy a new trackball or a different mouse; generally, these new toys require a bit of adjustment before you are comfortable with them.

DIFFICULTY LEVEL

Customize It ⁂

For precise work such as image editing or desktop publishing, you may want to temporarily slow your mouse tracking. Conversely, fast-action 3D games benefit from faster mouse tracking, and you are likely to benefit from a faster mouse pointer in your everyday applications.

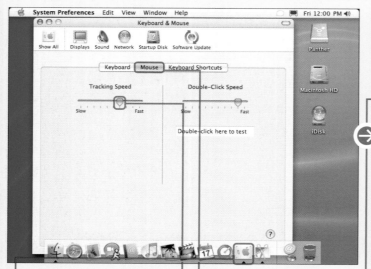
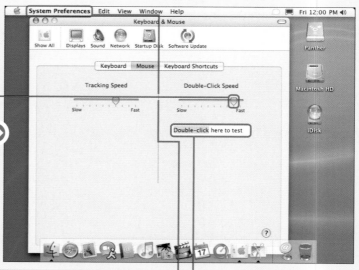

① Click the System Preferences icon in the dock.

○ The System Preferences dialog box appears.

② Click the Keyboard & Mouse icon.

③ Click Mouse.

④ Click the Tracking Speed slider and drag it to the speed that you want.

Note: This slider controls how fast your mouse pointer moves across your desktop when you move the mouse.

⑤ Click the Double-Click Speed slider and drag it to the speed that you want.

Note: This controls the speed to register a double-click. If your natural double-click speed does not always trigger a double-click, set this slider accordingly.

○ To test the double-click setting, try double-clicking in the Double-Click Here to Test box. If some of the text is highlighted, you have set your Double-Click Speed slider correctly.

⑥ Click System Preferences ⇨ Quit System Preferences.

5

Display or hide DESKTOP ICONS

#9

DIFFICULTY LEVEL

Panther offers you the choice of hiding certain icons that would normally appear on your Mac OS X desktop. If you would like to simplify your desktop for your kids or hide connected network servers from casual users, you are in the right place.

Customize It ☀

In the General Finder Preferences dialog box, you can specify whether a new Finder window displays the contents of your Home folder or your computer when you first open it. If several people use the same Macintosh, the Home folder option is probably the best; if you are the only person using your computer, I recommend the Computer option.

① Click the Finder icon in the dock.

○ The Finder menu is displayed.

② Click Finder.

③ Click Preferences.

○ The General Finder Preferences dialog box appears.

④ Click Hard Disks to hide all hard drive icons on your desktop (☑ changes to ☐).

⑤ Click CDs, DVDs and iPods to hide all CD, DVD, external hard drive, and Zip disk icons on your desktop (☑ changes to ☐).

⑥ Click Connected Servers to hide all network server icons on your desktop (☑ changes to ☐).

⑦ Click the Close button to save your changes.

Configure
VISUAL AND
AUDIO AIDS

Apple has recognized that not everyone has perfect vision or hearing. Today's larger monitors make it easy to configure Mac OS X so that your desktop and applications are easier to read; this cuts down on eye strain and helps prevent headaches after several hours at the keyboard. For those who cannot hear the system alert sounds, you can also set Panther to flash the screen instead.

In Panther, you can configure visual and audio aids in the Universal Access pane of the System Preferences dialog box. Do not be surprised if you

suddenly hear your Macintosh speaking to you while making changes to the settings in the Universal Access pane! If the Enable Text-to-Speech for Universal Access Preferences check box is enabled, Panther will automatically speak the name of each control on the pane when you move your mouse pointer over it. This only affects the controls on the Universal Access pane, so if you move to another pane within System Preferences, you will not hear the speech.

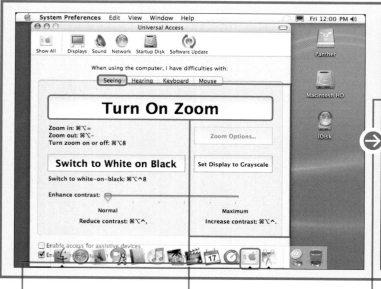

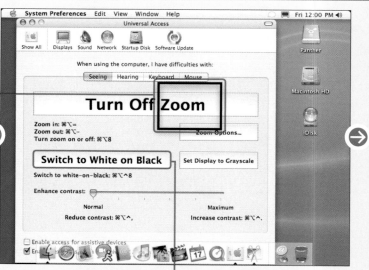

① Click the System Preferences icon in the dock.

○ The System Preferences dialog box appears.

② Click the Universal Access icon.

○ The Universal Access pane appears.

③ Click Seeing.

④ Click Turn On Zoom to enable the Zoom feature.

○ You can select a portion of the screen to zoom by moving the mouse, which moves the black window.

⑤ Press ⌘+Option+= to zoom in on the portion of the screen in the window.

⑥ Press ⌘+Option+- (the minus sign) to incrementally zoom out again.

⑦ Click Switch to White on Black to reverse these colors.

DIFFICULTY LEVEL

Did You Know? ☀

You do not have to open the Universal Access pane each time that you want to zoom in on a portion of the screen; you can just press ⌘+Option+8 at any time to turn zoom on, which will display the black zoom window. To turn zoom off again, press ⌘+Option+8.

Did You Know? ☀

If the black window does not appear when you turn on the Zoom feature in the Universal Access pane, you may need to configure the maximum zoom setting. Click the Zoom Options button and drag the Maximum Zoom control to a number higher than the default of 1. To zoom past the maximum or minimum settings, **hold down** (instead of press) ⌘+Option+= (the equals sign) or ⌘+Option+- (the minus sign).

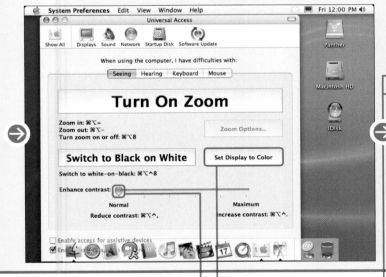

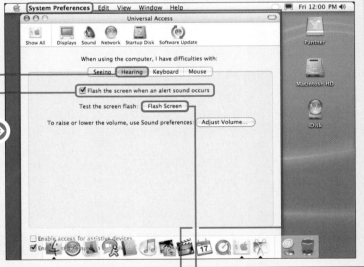

○ Panther creates a "negative desktop" that some Mac users find easier on the eyes.

○ You can switch between Black on White and White on Black by using the ⌘+Option+Control+8 key sequence.

⑧ Click Set Display to Grayscale to remove colors.

Note: This produces a display much like a grayscale photograph, which may help some Mac users who cannot easily distinguish colors.

⑨ Click and drag the Enhance Contrast slider to increase the contrast.

⑩ Click Hearing.

⑪ Click Flash the Screen When an Alert Sound Occurs to enable the check box (☐ changes to ☑).

○ To preview the flash effect, you can click Flash Screen.

⑫ Click System Preferences.

⑬ Click Quit System Preferences.

Customize the
FINDER

Because the Finder is the center of your Mac OS X Panther desktop, it is important that you learn how to customize it to your personal preferences. For example, some Mac users prefer the original Icon view, in which files and folders are represented as individual icons, whereas others prefer the List and Column views, in which files and folders are presented in indented lists.

Panther introduces the Finder Places sidebar (see Task 12 in Chapter 2) — the column on the left of the Finder window that holds both items, such as

files and folders, and devices, such as hard drives, removable USB drives, and CDs or DVDs. Click an item to open it; if the item is a document, Panther automatically runs the corresponding application for you. There is more to the Places sidebar, however: You will notice that it also allows you convenient access to a number of different locations, such as network servers, your Home folder, and your Applications folder.

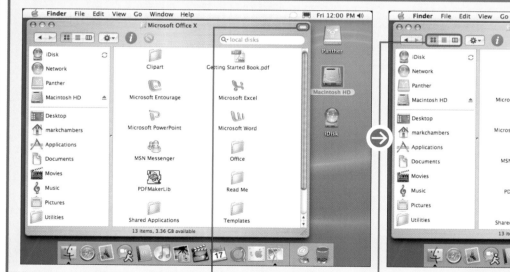

SWITCH VIEWS

① Press ⌘+N.

O Mac OS X displays a new Finder window.

② Click the toolbar button to show (or hide) the Finder toolbar.

③ Click the corresponding View button in the Finder toolbar to toggle between Icon, List, and Column view modes.

Note: Changing the view mode affects only the current location in your system — for example, the current folder or hard drive.

Did You Know? ※

You can click and drag the
divider bar to resize the list on
the left of the Finder window.

DIFFICULTY LEVEL

Customize It! ※

To make changes to all windows
displayed with a specific view
mode — like the size of the icons in
Icon view, or a default sorting order in
List view — choose the view mode that
you want to configure and press ⌘+J.
Make sure that you click All Windows to
apply your changes to any window displayed
in that mode.

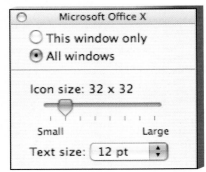

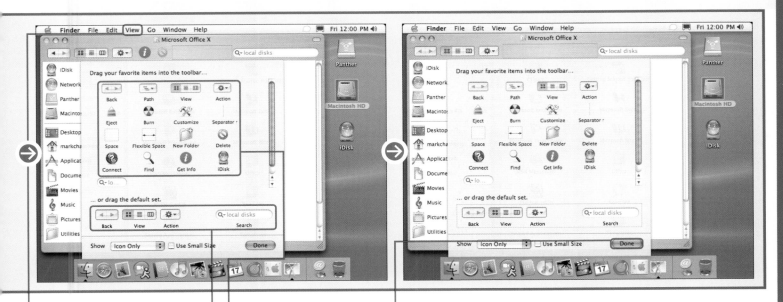

**ADD OR REMOVE
TOOLBAR BUTTONS**

④ Click View.

⑤ Click Customize Toolbar.

⑥ Drag buttons to and
from the toolbar to
customize it.

○ You can drag the default
toolbar button set as a whole
to reset your toolbar
configuration.

⑦ Click Done.

○ Your changes to the
toolbar are saved.

CHAPTER 2

Managing Files and Folders

The Finder has always been one of the most important aspects of the Mac OS. After all, this one often-copied feature set the Mac apart from its competition back in the early days of the personal computer. Panther continues in this tradition with many new Finder features that help make your file management much quicker and easier.

Some of the Finder improvements in Panther are updates to previous features; some are completely new features. Yet others are features that used to be in the Mac OS, but then disappeared, only to reappear in Panther.

For starters, the Finder has been totally revamped for Mac OS 10.3.

The first thing that you will notice is that Finder windows are metal in Panther, not the pinstripe look of Jaguar and earlier. Aesthetic issues aside, Finder windows have lots of new functionality. Every Finder window has a Places sidebar that gives you extraordinarily speedy access to nearly any location on your hard drive.

You can search for and locate files directly in Finder windows. Not only is this convenient in Panther, but it is also tremendously fast. To help you further organize your files, Panther reintroduces color labels and gives a much-needed facelift to the standard Open and Save dialog boxes.

TOP 100

#12   Accelerate file access with
Panther's new Places sidebar 22

#13   Use spring-loaded folders
to reduce clutter 24

#14   Access contextual menu commands 25

#15   Leverage keyboard shortcuts to speed
up work 26

#16   Find files in a flash 28

#17   Use color labels 29

#18   Access file information with Get Info 30

#19   Open a file without using the default
application 31

#20   Copy files four different ways 32

#21   Create an alias 34

#22   Customize icons of files and folders 36

#23   Navigate Panther's new Open
and Save dialog boxes 37

#24   Protect files from prying eyes 38

Accelerate file access with Panther's new
PLACES SIDEBAR

The first thing that you will notice about Panther is that Apple has made some significant changes to the Finder. Chief among these changes are improvements to Finder windows. Each Finder window now has a Places sidebar that displays drives, including hard drives, removable drives (such as CD and DVD), network drives, and even your iDisk. You can view the contents of any drive by clicking its icon in the Places sidebar. Its contents appear in the Content view. As you navigate through the folders on a drive, the Places sidebar remains constant. When you change between Icon, List, and Column views, the Places sidebar does not change.

You can customize the area below the drives in the Places sidebar with your own files and folders. As you add an item to the Places sidebar, the icons in the sidebar resize to accommodate the new addition until you reach the icons' minimum size.

Removing items from the Places sidebar is a simple drag-and-drop operation. When you drag items away from the Places sidebar, they disappear completely. If you have ever removed items from the dock, you will be at home with this operation.

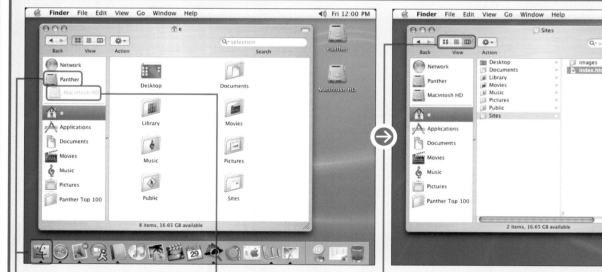

① Click the Finder icon in the dock.

② In the Finder window click a drive icon in the Places sidebar to view its contents.

③ Click and drag a drive icon in the Places sidebar to rearrange its position in the sidebar.

○ The other drive icons move to accommodate the new drive position.

④ Choose a view type for the window by clicking one of the three View icons.

○ The Places sidebar continues showing your drives and custom elements and the Content view changes.

Caution! ☀

When you remove an item
from the Places sidebar, it has no
effect on the item that it represents.
For example, removing a document from
the Places sidebar does not delete the actual
file or move it to the Trash. It simply removes
the item from the Places sidebar. If you are
familiar with older versions of the Mac OS,
items in the Places sidebar work somewhat like
aliases or items in the toolbar. If you remove one,
you can always re-create it later.

Did You Know? ☀

The Places sidebar is an optional aspect of the
Panther Finder. If you prefer the Finder style of
older Mac operating systems, simply drag the
vertical handle beside the Places sidebar to the left.
When the handle meets the left edge of the window,
the Places sidebar disappears.

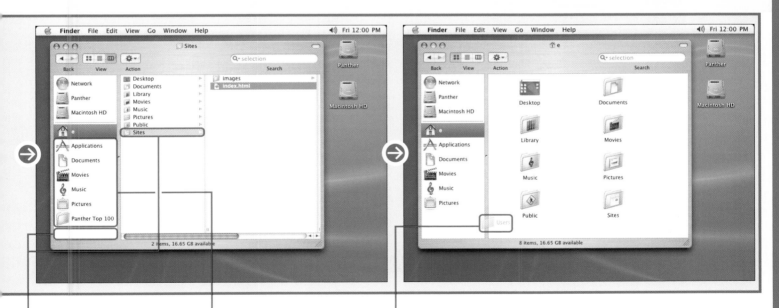

⑤ Drag the files and folders that you use most often to the bottom of the Places sidebar for convenient one-click access.

○ The Places sidebar icons resize to accommodate the new additions.

⑥ Click and drag the icons at the bottom of the Places sidebar to arrange them to your whim.

⑦ Click and drag an icon from the bottom of the Places sidebar to anywhere outside of the sidebar.

○ The icon is removed from the Places sidebar.

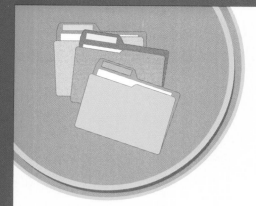

Use SPRING-LOADED FOLDERS
to reduce clutter

To move a file or folder between two locations usually means that you have to be able to see both locations — the origin of the file or folder and the destination to which you want to move it. This tends to clutter the desktop quickly, particularly if you want to move more than one file or folder.

Spring-loaded folders help alleviate this problem. To move a file using spring-loaded folders, simply drag the file onto a folder, but do not let go of the mouse button. After a brief pause, the folder will pop open, displaying its contents. You can continue to navigate

this way as long as you continue to press the mouse button. When you arrive at the destination that you want, let go of the mouse button, and the file moves to the destination folder.

You can adjust the amount of time that you have to wait until spring-loaded folders open in the Finder Preferences dialog box. You can also remove the wait altogether by pressing the spacebar as soon as you drag an icon to a folder.

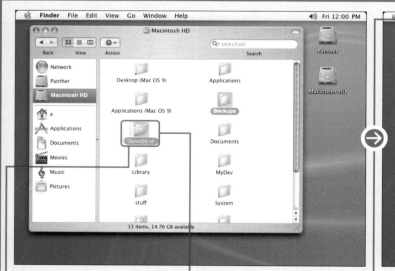

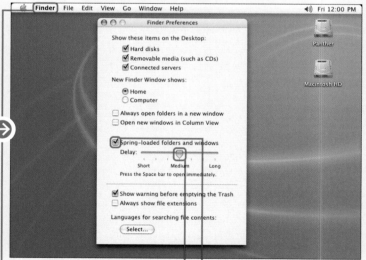

MOVE FILES

① Open the Finder.

② Locate a file to move.

③ Drag it onto a folder or drive icon, making sure not to release the mouse button.

○ After a brief pause, the folder opens.

④ Let go of the mouse button.

⑤ Repeat steps **2** to **4**, but this time, press the spacebar instead of waiting.

○ There is no pause; the folder opens immediately.

⑥ Let go of the mouse button.

CHANGE SPRING-LOADED FOLDER PREFERENCES

⑦ Click Finder.

⑧ Click Preferences.

○ The Finder Preferences dialog box opens.

⑨ Click Spring-Loaded Folders and Windows to turn the spring-loaded feature on or off.

○ You can move the Delay slider to adjust the amount of time that you must wait until a spring-loaded folder or window opens.

Access CONTEXTUAL MENU commands

14

Because most Macintosh computers have a mouse with one button, some people mistakenly believe that the Mac OS does not have a right-click mechanism. If you are using a Macintosh with a one-button mouse or a trackpad, holding the Control key while clicking opens a menu with items that correspond to the context of the click. For example, if you Control+click a document, you will see a pop-up menu that pertains to documents. Likewise, Control+clicking a folder opens a menu for folders.

Apply It

Typically, you will Control+click files and folders to perform some operation with a contextual menu, but you do not need to Control+click a file or folder to see a contextual menu. You can also Control+click the desktop or the dock itself to reveal a contextual menu that applies to the desktop.

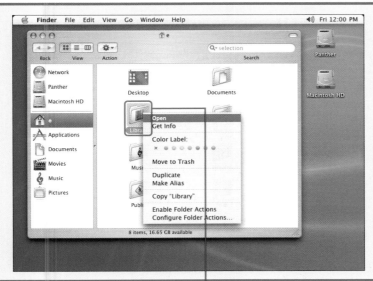

ACCESS FINDER CONTEXTUAL MENUS

① Open a Finder window.

② Press and hold the Control key.

③ While continuing to hold the Control key, click a file or folder.

○ A contextual menu appears with functions in it that apply to the item that you clicked.

ACCESS SAFARI CONTEXTUAL MENUS

① Launch the Safari Web browser.

② Load a Web page.

③ Control+click the Web page to reveal a contextual menu that applies to Web pages.

④ Control+click a link on the Web page to view a menu that pertains to links.

Note: Safari is not the only application that supports contextual menus. Try Control+clicking in various applications to see what else is available.

Leverage
KEYBOARD SHORTCUTS
to speed up work

Despite the ease of use that you gain from a mouse, sometimes using a keyboard is faster. To this end, the Mac OS includes all kinds of useful keyboard shortcuts. The base key for keyboard shortcuts is the Command key (⌘). In addition to the ⌘ key, keyboard shortcuts often use other modifier keys such as Option and Shift. Using the ⌘ key and some other combination of keys, you can perform nearly every operation on your Mac without ever touching the mouse.

The Finder is one of the biggest supporters of keyboard shortcuts. You can find many of these shortcuts by reading the shortcuts displayed in each menu of the Finder.

In addition to the default keyboard shortcuts available in the Finder and other applications, you can also create your own custom keyboard shortcuts via the Keyboard pane of the System Preferences dialog box.

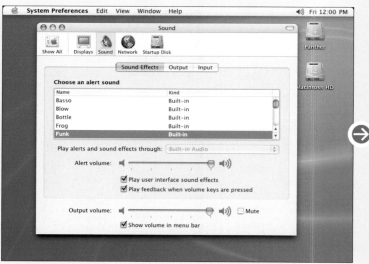

TOGGLE BETWEEN DOCK APPLICATIONS

① Press ⌘+Tab to switch to the next application in the dock.

○ The application-switching window appears with the active application highlighted.

② Repeatedly press ⌘+Tab to cycle through each of the open applications.

③ Press ⌘+Shift+Tab to switch the applications in the opposite direction.

OPEN DIFFERENT SYSTEM PREFERENCES PANES

① Press Option and one of the speaker buttons on the keyboard.

○ The System Preferences dialog box's Sound pane opens.

② Press Option and either F15 or F14.

○ The System Preferences switches to the Displays pane.

Note: These keyboard shortcuts work if the System Preferences dialog box is already open or is closed.

Customize It!

You can really hotrod your Mac like never before with the custom keyboard shortcuts in the Keyboard Shortcuts pane of Systems Preferences. It is here where you can toggle premade keyboard shortcuts on and off. You can also change the keyboard combinations that make the shortcuts function. Furthermore, by clicking the Add Keyboard Shortcut button, you can create your own keyboard shortcuts.

Did You Know?

New Macintosh keyboards lack a Power key, as was in vogue for years on Macintosh keyboards. This does not mean, however, that you cannot still have the same functionality as when the keyboards did have Power keys; you can press Control+Eject to make the standard Shutdown window appear. However, to start up your Mac, you are still relegated to pushing the button on the machine itself.

DIFFICULTY LEVEL

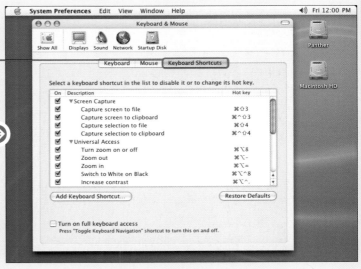

ACCESS KEYBOARD SHORTCUT OPTIONS

③ Click Show All.

○ The System Preferences dialog box displays all the installed Preferences panes.

④ Click Keyboard & Mouse.

○ The Keyboard & Mouse pane appears.

⑤ Click Keyboard Shortcuts.

○ The Keyboard Shortcuts section of the Keyboard & Mouse Preferences pane appears, where you can change your keyboard shortcut settings.

FIND FILES
in a flash

Macintosh operating systems have always been good at helping you find files on your hard drive. Panther takes these features one step further, offering nearly instantaneous searches.

Every Finder window now has a Search field like iTunes. This permits you to search for files from wherever you are in the Finder. By clicking the magnifying lens icon next to the Search field, you can direct your search towards specific locations.

Of course, you can always use the traditional Find window by pressing ⌘+F.

Did You Know? ☀

The search/find functions used to appear in the Sherlock application. They no longer appear there, as Sherlock has become solely an Internet tool since Mac OS X 10.2.

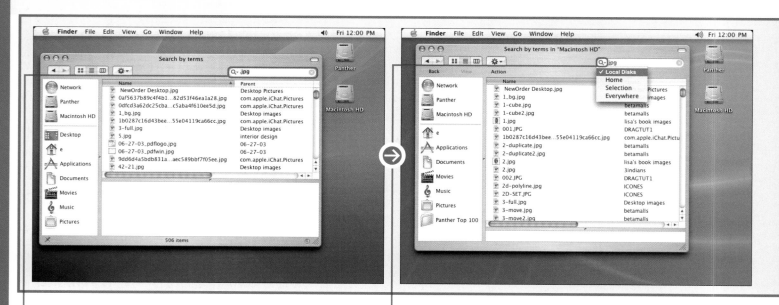

① Open a new Finder window.

② Type some text in the Search field.

○ Your Mac begins searching for files the second that you press a key. As you continue typing, the search further refines itself based on what you have typed.

③ Click the magnifying lens icon.

○ A menu opens, offering you choices of where to search for files.

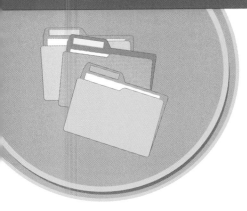

Use color
LABELS

Labels offer a set of colors that you can attach to a file or folder to denote your own form of colorized organization. Suppose, for example, that you would like to sort files in a particular folder based on how important they are. Your Mac does not know how important one file is over another. By using labels, you can assign a scale of importance to your files. After you have assigned an importance to each of the files, it is straightforward to sort them by that importance.

Did You Know? ☀

For years, Macintosh users were accustomed to sorting their files in the Finder by name, date, type, and label. Then, one day labels died. Mac OS X 10.0 through 10.2 lacked the label feature. Panther reintroduces labels in a new-and-improved form.

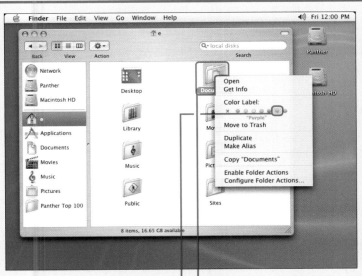

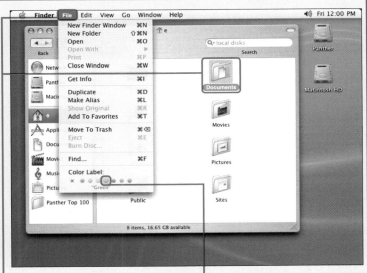

LABEL WITH A CONTEXTUAL MENU

① Open a Finder window that has files and/or folders in it that you would like to sort.

② Control+click the file or folder.

○ A contextual menu appears.

③ Under Color Label, click a color to represent some criterion for the file.

LABEL WITH THE FILE MENU

① In a Finder window, click to select a file or folder.

② Click File.

③ Click a color under Color Label to change the color for the file.

○ The file is now labeled with the color that you specified.

Access file information with GET INFO

#18

DIFFICULTY LEVEL

Finder windows give you a lot of information about files and folders, but they reveal only a fraction of what is possible. By opening the Get Info window for a file or folder, you can learn about and alter a variety of information.

The Get Info window displays information about files and folders contextually, which is to say that it displays specific data depending on what the file or folder is. You can view and change all sorts of information about a file or folder, including its name, size, type, date modified, date created, file extension, icon, permissions, and comments.

Caution! ※

Be very careful if you change permissions on a file; otherwise, some user may not be able to use it later. Changing permissions on files requires a user with the appropriate rights to do so.

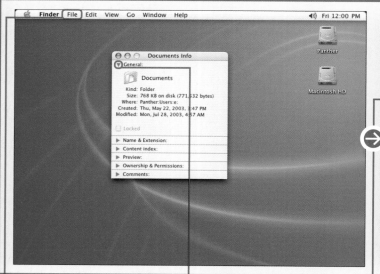

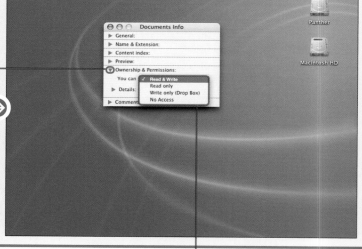

① In the Finder, select a file or folder by clicking it.

② Click File.

③ Click Get Info.

○ The Get Info window opens.

④ Click a disclosure triangle to expand that portion of the Get Info window.

⑤ Click the Ownership & Permissions disclosure triangle to see which users can read and write to the file or folder.

○ If you have an appropriate account, you can change the permissions for the file or folder.

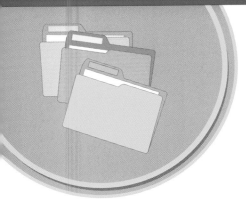

OPEN A FILE
without using the default application

DIFFICULTY LEVEL

When you double-click a file in the Finder, it usually launches an application that can handle that type of file. This works fine for most day-to-day tasks, but sometimes it is not what you want. Suppose, for example, that you have a JPEG file that you downloaded from the Internet using Safari. Perhaps all your JPEG icons display an icon based on the Preview application. When you want to edit the image that you downloaded with another application

such as Adobe Photoshop, you usually have to jump through some hoops to make the image open in the other application.

Fortunately, Panther takes away some of the guesswork. You can instantly change which application will open a file. You can also tell your Mac to open all files of that type with the application of your choosing.

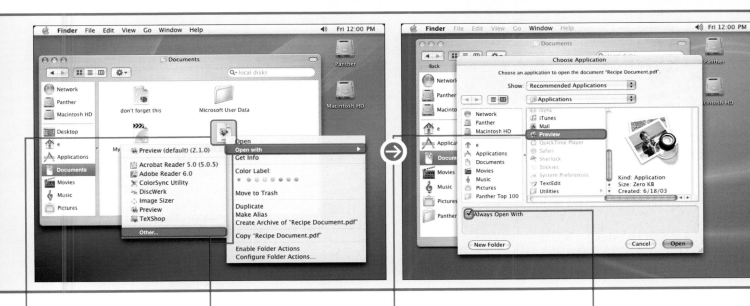

① Control+click a file to open a contextual menu and see what application will open when you double-click that type of file.

Note: If you have another application that can open the file, you can change to that one.

② Click Open With.

③ Click Other.

○ The Choose Application dialog box opens.

④ Select an application and click OK.

○ Alternatively, you can click Always Open With to make all documents of this type launch with the newly selected application (☐ changes to ☑).

COPY FILES
four different ways

Copying files is one of the most important operations that you will perform in the Finder. Copying files is so important that the Mac OS gives you four different ways to do it. Whether you choose to use the keyboard shortcut, the contextual menu's Duplicate item, the mouse and keyboard shortcut, or the Copy, Edit, and Paste menu items, copying files is vital for making backups, experimenting with a file without ruining it, and other tasks.

In addition to the specific copying tasks, the Finder sometimes copies automatically for you. For example, if you drag a file from one disk to another, the Finder assumes that you want to make a copy on the destination drive. On the other hand, if you drag a file from one place on a drive to another location on the same drive, the Finder moves the file; no copy operation takes place.

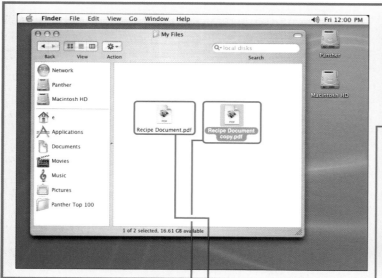

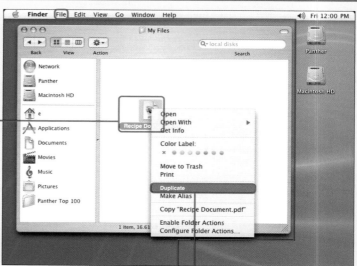

USE A KEYBOARD SHORTCUT

① Open a Finder window and navigate to a file or folder that you would like to copy.

② Select the file or folder by clicking it.

③ Press ⌘+D.

○ The Finder creates a copy of the file in the same location as the original.

USE A MENU

① Control+click a file or folder that you would like to copy.

○ A contextual menu appears over the file or folder.

② Click Duplicate.

○ Alternatively, you can click File ➪ Duplicate.

○ The Finder creates a copy of the original file or folder in the same location as the original.

Apply It ※

All the copy operations described in this task work for both one file as well as multiple files. To copy multiple files, first select them in the Finder and then perform a copy operation by Option+dragging, copying via the contextual menu, or pressing ⌘+D.

Did You Know? ※

Everyone makes mistakes, so the Finder can compensate for that. To help you out of a jam, the Undo function works in the Finder, too. If you make a mistake, press ⌘+Z. The Finder immediately undoes any damage that you may have done. This is handy for times when you accidentally copy files to the wrong location.

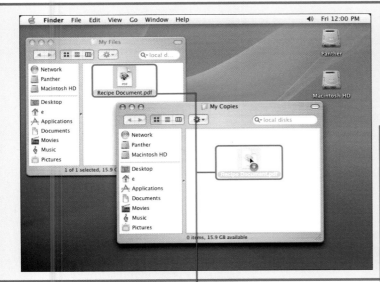

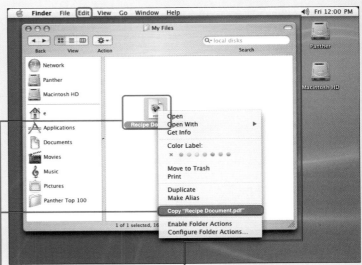

USE THE OPTION KEY AND DRAGGING

① Press and hold the Option key.

② Drag the file that you would like to copy to a destination location.

○ The Finder creates a copy of the file in the destination that you designated.

USE COPY, EDIT, AND PASTE

① Control+click the file or folder to copy.

○ A contextual menu appears.

② Click Copy "*Filename*," where *Filename* is the name of the file.

③ Navigate to a destination folder in the Finder.

④ Click Edit.

⑤ Click Paste.

○ The Finder creates a copy of the file in the destination of your choice.

Create an
ALIAS

Mac OS X places files all over your hard drive in a maze of folders. Sometimes it is simply inconvenient to hunt down a commonly used file or folder. To make your life easier, the Mac OS gives you aliases. *Aliases* are special files that do not do anything except point to another file or folder. They are not copies of the file or folder. They have only one purpose — to show you where a file is. Rather than dig through folders looking for a file that you use all the time, you can create an alias for it and place

that alias somewhere convenient, such as your desktop or Favorites folder. Then, when you want to open that file or folder, all you have to do is double-click its alias.

Aliases can also reveal the location of the file or folder that they represent. This is especially handy for locating the original file very quickly, or even as a navigation tool to go to the folder that contains the aliased file or folder.

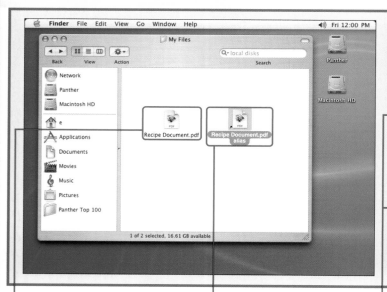

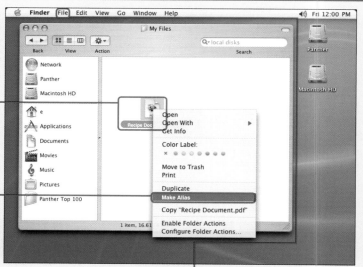

USE A KEYBOARD SHORTCUT

① Click to select a file or folder in the Finder.

② Press ⌘+L.

○ The Finder creates an alias that points to the file or folder.

③ Move the alias to someplace convenient for easy access to the original file or folder.

USE A MENU

① Control+click a file or folder in the Finder.

○ A contextual menu appears.

② Click Make Alias.

○ Alternatively, you can click File ➪ Make Alias.

○ The Finder creates an alias for the file or folder.

③ Drag the newly created alias to the location that you want.

Did You Know? ※

Aliases are superintelligent.
You can safely move the file or
folder that an alias points to without
breaking the alias. Instead of pointing
to a specific location, an alias tracks its
master much as you track a stolen car
with a GPS device.

Apply It ※

Besides the usual aliases in the Finder, the dock
has it own aliaslike functionality. Click and hold
an application icon to reveal a Show in Finder
contextual menu item. This can be especially useful
if you want to navigate quickly to that application's
parent folder.

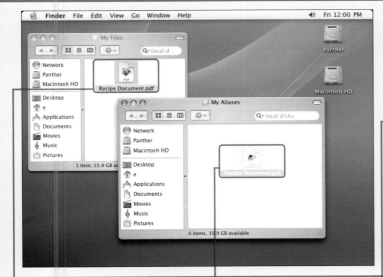

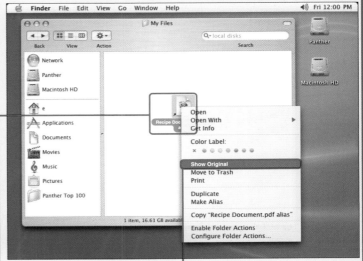

USE KEYS AND DRAGGING

① Click to select a file or folder in the Finder.

② Press and hold the ⌘ and Option keys.

③ Drag the file or folder to a new location.

○ The Finder creates an alias to the file in the destination of your choice.

LOCATE AN ALIAS'S TARGET FILE OR FOLDER

① Locate an alias in the Finder.

② Control+click the alias.

○ A contextual menu appears.

③ Click Show Original.

○ A Finder window opens, showing the location of the original file or folder that the alias represents.

35

CUSTOMIZE ICONS
of files and folders

As has been the case for years in the Mac OS, you can customize the icon of any file or folder in the Finder. Icons are a vital component of the graphical user interface. They help you quickly identify files and folders without having to read a filename. Many items on your hard drive have uniquely identifiable icons. To those that do not, however, you can assign a custom icon; this will continue to save you time far into the future.

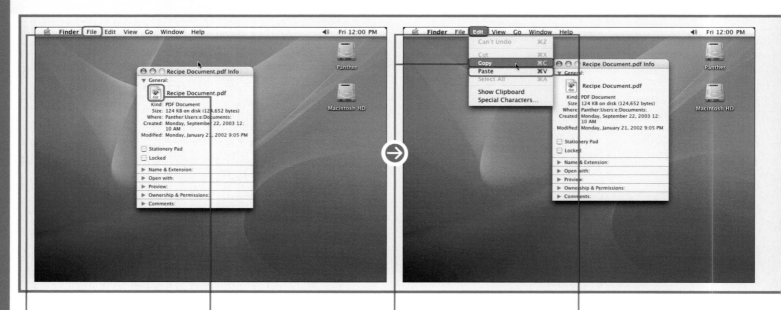

① Choose a file or folder in the Finder whose icon you would like to use.

② Click File.

③ Click Get Info.

○ The Get Info window opens.

④ Click the icon at the top of the Get Info window.

⑤ Click Edit.

⑥ Click Copy.

⑦ Click a file or folder in the Finder whose icon you would like to change.

⑧ Open the Get Info window for the file or folder.

⑨ Click Edit.

⑩ Click Paste.

○ The icon of the file or folder changes.

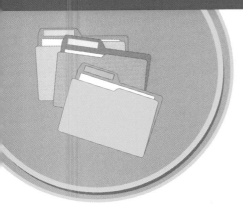

Navigate Panther's new OPEN AND SAVE DIALOG boxes

#23

DIFFICULTY LEVEL

When Mac OS X first arrived on the scene, many people were optimistic about the operating system. Two features that seemed ripe for change from previous versions of the OS were the standard Open and Save dialog boxes. Unfortunately, some were disappointed in what they saw in Mac OS 10.0, 10.1, and 10.2. With Panther (OS X 10.3), Apple has finally redeemed itself by completely revamping the Open and Save dialog boxes.

Resembling the new Finder windows in Panther, the Open and Save dialog boxes offer significant improvements over previous versions. Gone is the extralong Favorites menu of earlier Mac OS X versions. Moreover, the dialog boxes support List and Column views as well as one-click access to your most often used places via the embedded Places sidebar.

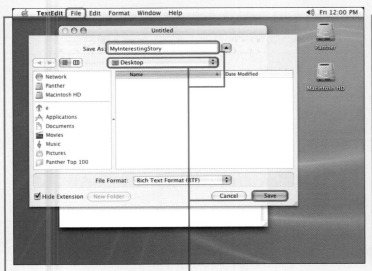

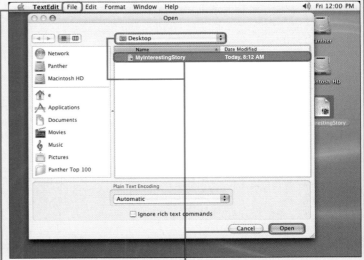

USE THE SAVE DIALOG BOX

(1) Launch an application such as TextEdit.

(2) Add some text to the document.

(3) Click File.

(4) Click Save.

○ The standard Save dialog box appears.

(5) Type a name.

(6) Navigate to the location where you would like to save the file just as you would in the Finder.

(7) Click Save.

○ The document is saved.

USE THE OPEN DIALOG BOX

(1) Click File.

(2) Click Open.

○ The Open dialog box appears.

(3) Navigate to the location of the file that you would like to open.

(4) Click the filename.

(5) Click Open.

○ The file opens.

PROTECT FILES
from prying eyes

Panther brings some significant new security features to Mac OS X. Chief among these features is FileVault. FileVault protects your files with strong encryption. FileVault encrypts all files contained within your Home directory. You will not even notice that the encryption is happening because Panther performs that operation on-the-fly. Later, when you want to open a protected file, Panther decrypts it as it opens it. You can access your encrypted files as long as you are logged in as a valid user.

If you forget your personal password, you may not be able to retrieve your files. To remedy this situation, you can set a master password that will unlock FileVault.

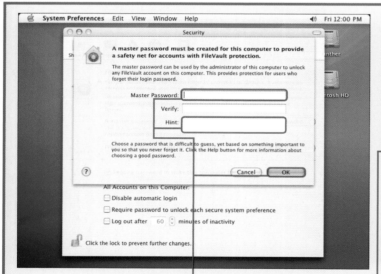

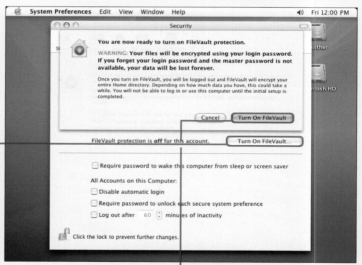

SET MASTER PASSWORD

① Open System Preferences.

② Click Security.

○ The Security pane appears.

③ Click Set Master Password.

○ A dialog box appears.

④ Type the password.

⑤ Type a hint to remind you about the password.

⑥ Click OK.

○ The master password is set.

ACTIVATE FILEVAULT

① Open System Preferences.

② Click Security.

③ Click Turn On FileVault.

○ FileVault prompts you for a password.

④ Type the password.

○ FileVault asks you again if you want to activate file encryption.

⑤ Click Turn On FileVault to activate it.

Note: As soon as you turn on FileVault, Panther logs you out and begins encrypting your Home directory. After it is encrypted, you can log in again.

Did You Know? ※

Panther uses 128-bit encryption. This means that it is very complicated for anyone to crack because there are trillions upon trillions of possible combinations that a hacker would have to try to break through the security. With today's computing power, this is impossible, and it appears that it will stay that way for years to come.

DIFFICULTY LEVEL

Apply It ※

File encryption is particularly useful for laptop owners. If you lose your laptop, you can at least be certain that no one will be able to steal your important business secrets, read your personal e-mails, or copy your homework. If you use a desktop computer at home, you may be less worried about someone looking at your files.

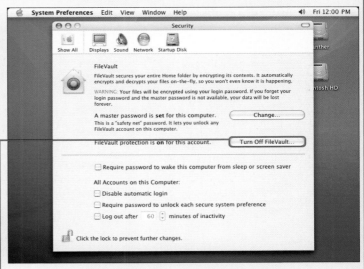

IDENTIFY WHEN FILEVAULT IS ACTIVE

① Open a new Finder window.

② Locate your Home directory in the Places sidebar.

○ When FileVault is active, the Home directory displays a silver icon of a house with a vault lock on it.

DEACTIVATE FILEVAULT

① Open System Preferences.

② Click Security.

③ Click Turn Off FileVault.

○ FileVault prompts you for a password.

④ Type the password.

○ FileVault asks you again if you want to deactivate file encryption.

⑤ Click Turn Off FileVault to deactivate it.

Note: As soon as you turn off FileVault, Panther logs you out and begins decrypting your Home directory. After it is decrypted, you can log in again.

CHAPTER 3

Using Panther More Efficiently

A car may actually have only three basic controls — a steering wheel, brake pedal, and accelerator pedal — but how you *use* those controls makes a big difference! It is the same with the basic controls within Mac OS X. Anyone can use the dock to launch or switch between applications, but there is hidden power there that can also help you work more efficiently with Panther and your applications. The same holds true for keyboard shortcuts, the Finder window, and the Go menu.

One new feature in Panther deserves a special mention: I have been very impressed by Exposé, which can literally save you dozens of keystrokes or mouse clicks a day if you run a large number of applications simultaneously. With Exposé, you press a single key and click the application window that you want.

In this chapter, you will find out how to configure this great efficiency feature.

In this chapter, I demonstrate some of the tricks that can help you speed through your daily tasks on your Macintosh. You will find tips on adding your favorite applications, items, and Web sites to the dock, and I will show you how to resize the dock and move it to a new position on your desktop. You will also learn how to specify which applications should start automatically when you load certain types of CDs or DVDs. This chapter also covers how to set your Mac to start or shut down automatically at certain times and how to allow other users to access your computer without your having to log out.

TOP 100

#25 Add and delete dock icons 42

#26 Add Web sites to the dock 43

#27 Customize the Finder toolbar 44

#28 Relocate and resize the dock 45

#29 Configure Exposé 46

#30 Launch recent items 47

#31 Put your Mac to sleep 48

#32 Switch between users 49

#33 Start or shut down your Mac automatically 50

#34 Hide and display the Finder toolbar 51

#35 Use the Go menu 52

#36 Save time with keyboard shortcuts 53

#37 Work automatically with CD and
DVD discs 54

#38 Use Mac OS X services 55

#39 View files with Preview 56

Add and delete
DOCK ICONS

DIFFICULTY LEVEL

The dock is a great launching pad for applications and documents, but you do not have to settle for the default set of icons. You can customize the dock with the applications and documents that you use most often. You can even remove the default icons that you do not use. With a few seconds' work, you no longer have to open a Finder window or create an alias on your desktop to enjoy quick and easy access to the tools that you need throughout a computing session.

Did You Know? ※

You can add a folder to the right side of the dock — the portion of the dock on the right side of the vertical line. To view the contents of a folder in the dock, move your mouse cursor on top of the folder icon and then click and hold your mouse button to display a pop-up menu. You can click any item in the pop-up menu to launch it.

ADD A DOCK ICON

1 Drag the item's icon from the Finder window to the dock.

○ The icon is added to the dock.

REMOVE A DOCK ICON

1 Drag the icon from the dock and drop it anywhere on your desktop.

○ The icon is removed from the dock.

Add
WEB SITES
to the dock

#26

DIFFICULTY LEVEL

Do you have a favorite Web site that you visit several times a day? If so, you can check that Web page with a single click by adding the site to your dock, where it will appear with an @ icon. When you click the @, Panther automatically launches Safari, connects to the Internet, if necessary, and loads the site. The default dock arrangement already includes a Web site: the Mac OS X main page on Apple's Web site at www.apple.com.

Did You Know? ☀

When you minimize a Safari window, a miniature thumbnail of the Web page appears in the dock.

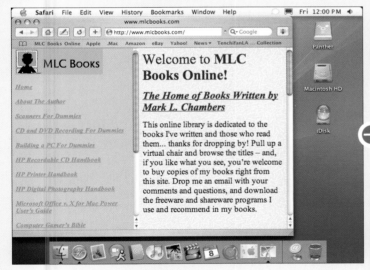

① Open Safari and navigate to the Web page that you want.

② Drag the URL icon from the Address bar to the right side of the dock.

○ The Web page is added to the dock.

Customize the
FINDER
TOOLBAR

DIFFICULTY LEVEL

The Finder window is the most often-used tool in Panther — so it is a good idea to customize the controls that it carries. Panther enables you to add and remove controls from the Finder window toolbar, making it easy to fine-tune the Finder for maximum efficiency.

Customize It ※

You can choose to display just text labels on your Finder toolbar; to do so, in the Customize Toolbar dialog box, click the Show drop-down list and click Text Only.

Customize It ※

To reduce the space taken by icons in the Finder toolbar, in the Customize Toolbar dialog box, click the Use Small Size check box to enable it.

① Press ⌘+N.

○ Panther displays a new Finder window.

② Click View.

③ Click Customize Toolbar.

○ Panther displays the Customize Toolbar dialog box.

④ Drag the items from the list that you want into the Finder window toolbar.

○ A rectangle appears to indicate where the item can be placed.

⑤ To remove an item, drag it from the toolbar onto the desktop.

⑥ Click the Show drop-down list and click Icon Only to turn toolbar labels off.

⑦ When you have finished modifying the toolbar, click Done.

○ Your changes appear on the toolbar.

RELOCATE AND RESIZE
the dock

#28

DIFFICULTY LEVEL

You are not locked into using the dock at the bottom of the desktop; you can move the dock to the right or left side of the desktop, if you prefer. You can also change the size of the icons in the dock whenever you want. For example, if you would like to add a large number of items to the dock, you can resize it to make it smaller to accommodate them.

Did You Know? ※

You can elect to hide the dock entirely from the Dock pane in System Preferences. To do so, click the Automatically Hide and Show the Dock check box to enable it. The dock disappears, but you can display it at any time by moving your mouse cursor all the way to the corresponding edge of the screen.

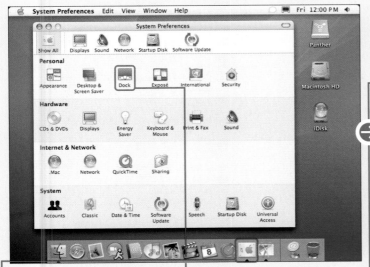

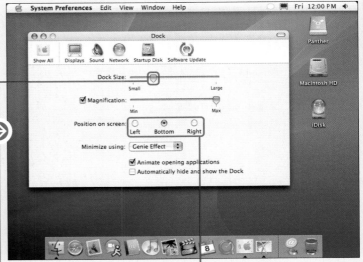

① Click the System Preferences icon in the dock.

○ The System Preferences window appears.

② Click Dock.

○ The Dock settings appear.

③ Drag the Dock Size slider to resize the dock icons.

④ Click Left, Bottom, or Right to specify where the dock should appear (○ changes to ◉).

⑤ Press ⌘+Q to quit System Preferences and save your changes.

Configure EXPOSÉ

DIFFICULTY LEVEL

Exposé is a new feature in Panther that is designed to make switching between applications much easier — especially when you are running a large number of applications simultaneously. The feature can be controlled through both keyboard shortcuts and activation/deactivation *corners* that you specify in System Preferences. Moving your mouse cursor to the specified corner activates the chosen Exposé command.

By default, you can display all your application windows at one time by pressing and holding the F9 key. To display only the active windows for the current application, press and hold F10. Finally, you can press and hold F11 to move all application windows to the edges of the screen.

Did You Know? ※

Screen corners can also be used to turn on (or disable) your screen saver. These command options appear in both the Exposé pane and the Desktop & Screen Saver pane.

 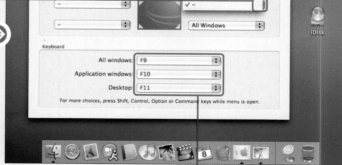

(1) Click the System Preferences icon in the dock.

○ The System Preferences window appears.

(2) Click Exposé.

○ The Exposé settings appear.

(3) Click the drop-down list box at the corner to set.

(4) Click the command to assign to that corner.

Note: For example, you can select All Windows; when you move your mouse cursor to that corner, all the windows will be displayed.

(5) Click the three Keyboard drop-down list boxes to specify new Exposé keyboard shortcuts.

(6) Press ⌘+Q to quit System Preferences and save your changes.

Launch
RECENT ITEMS

#30

DIFFICULTY LEVEL

Most Mac owners tend to work on the same documents and use the same applications many times over the course of a day — so Panther automatically keeps track of what you are using and what you are working on in the Recent Items list. It is much more efficient to use the Recent Items list to open a document or launch an application that you have used just an hour ago because you do not have to locate the document or application icon in the Finder window.

Did You Know? ※

You can clear the contents of the Recent Items list whenever you like; this is a good idea if you are switching projects or taking a notebook on the road. Display the Recent Items list and click the Clear Menu item at the bottom of the list. If your Recent Items list is long enough to scroll, move your mouse cursor on top of the arrow at the bottom of the list to scroll downward.

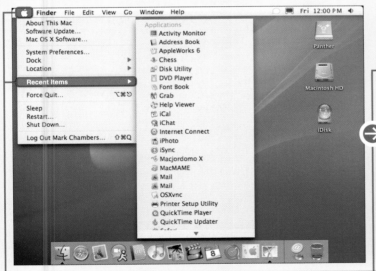

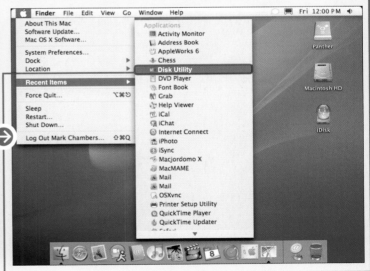

① Click .

② Move your mouse cursor on top of Recent Items.

○ The most recent items appear, sorted into an Applications group and a Documents group.

③ Click the application or document that you want.

○ The application is launched, or the document opens.

Put your Mac to
SLEEP

DIFFICULTY LEVEL

Do you turn your Macintosh off each time that you leave your desk? If you will return in a couple of hours, it is much more efficient to put your Mac to sleep instead because it takes far less time for Panther to return from sleep mode than to start up. Plus, your Mac can continue to run some applications while it is asleep, using very little power.

Did You Know? ☀

If your Mac's keyboard has a Media Eject key, you can hold down Control while you press the Media Eject key to display a confirmation dialog box, from which you can elect to put to sleep, restart, or shut down your Mac.

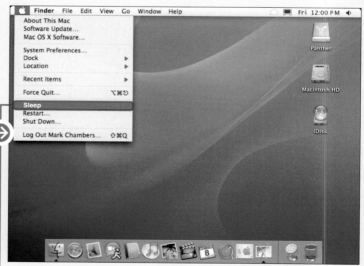

① Click .

② Click Sleep.

○ Your Mac blanks its screen and turns off the hard drive (when possible).

③ To wake up your Mac, press any of the arrow keys.

SWITCH between USERS

DIFFICULTY LEVEL

Do you share your Mac with others — perhaps in an office or a classroom environment? If so, you are likely to be stuck sitting idle while another user finishes a session. With Panther's new fast-user-switching feature, however, you can log in temporarily even if someone is already logged in with another account — perhaps to just print one of your documents or quickly check your e-mail. When you are finished, the original user can switch back to the original session without losing any documents or shutting down any applications.

To turn on fast user switching, use an Admin-level account to open System Preferences. Open the Accounts pane, click the Login Options button, and click the Enable Fast User Switching check box. Panther displays the current user at the right side of the Finder menu whenever fast user switching is turned on.

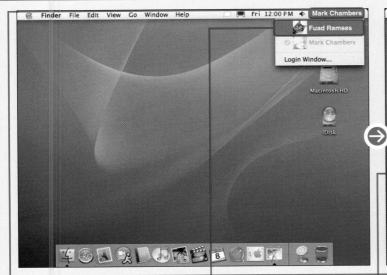

① Click the current username on the Finder menu.

○ The User Switch menu is displayed.

② Click the account name to which you want to switch.

○ Panther prompts you for the new user's login password.

③ Type the password and press Return.

○ Panther logs the new user in and displays his or her desktop.

START
or shut down your Mac
AUTOMATICALLY

#33

Would you like your Macintosh ready and waiting for you when you reach your home or office? How about leaving your Mac on when you leave and allowing it to turn itself off? Using your Mac's built-in clock, Panther can start up or shut down your computer automatically on a regular schedule.

If you combine this feature with Panther's capability to automatically log in a specific account and automatically launch Startup items for that account, you can walk into your office

and be greeted with Word, iCal, or Apple Mail already running!

DIFFICULTY LEVEL

Did You Know? ☀

By default, your Macintosh remains off if you are hit by a power failure — however, you can specify that Panther should restart your Mac automatically after a power failure. From the Energy Saver pane, click the Options button and then click the Restart Automatically after a Power Failure check box to enable it.

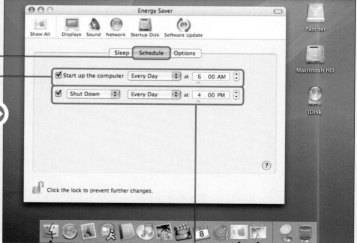

① Click the System Preferences icon in the dock.

○ The System Preferences window appears.

② Click Energy Saver.

○ The Energy Saver settings appear.

③ Click Schedule.

④ Click Start Up the Computer (☐ changes to ☑) and specify the recurrence and the time of day.

⑤ Click the second check box (☐ changes to ☑), choose Shut Down, and specify the recurrence and the time of day.

⑥ Press ⌘+Q to quit System Preferences and save your changes.

HIDE
and display the
FINDER
TOOLBAR

#34

DIFFICULTY LEVEL

Need more screen real estate to display a large number of files in the Finder window? Here is a trick that is popular among Apple power users: You can hide the Finder window toolbar when you are not using the toolbar buttons, which expands the area available for displaying items while shrinking the actual size of the window. When you hide the toolbar, the Finder Places sidebar also disappears, giving the window a rather lean, Spartan look.

Did You Know? ☀

You can always minimize a Finder window by double-clicking on the title bar.

HIDE THE TOOLBAR

① Click the toolbar button in the Finder window.

Note: Alternatively, you can press ⌘+Option+T.

○ The toolbar and Places sidebar disappear.

DISPLAY THE TOOLBAR

② Click the toolbar button again.

○ The toolbar and Places sidebar reappear.

Use the
GO MENU

Think of Panther's Go menu as a shortcut to all sorts of locations — both those on your local hard drives and those on external sources, such as your network or the Internet. The Go menu is a great one-stop solution to increasing your efficiency within Mac OS X.

Apple includes a number of the most commonly used locations as default choices on the Go menu, including your Home folder, iDisk, local network, and Applications folder. You can also use the Recent Folder submenu to quickly jump to folders that you have used in the recent past.

DIFFICULTY LEVEL

Did You Know? ※

If a Finder window is currently open, you can back up to the parent folder for your current location by pressing ⌘+up arrow or by clicking the Go menu and choosing the Enclosing Folder menu item.

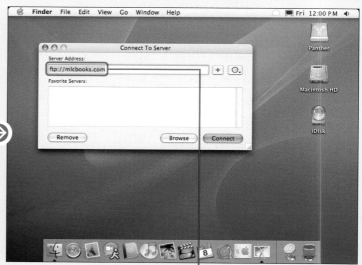

① Click Go.

② Click the destination that you want.

○ Click Home to jump to your Home folder.

○ Click iDisk to open your iDisk or display another .Mac user's iDisk or Public folder.

○ Click Recent Folders to jump to a folder that you have used in the recent past.

○ Click Connect to Server to connect to an FTP or file server across your local network or the Internet.

○ If you choose an option that requires more specific information, such as Connect to Server, a window appears asking for the exact location — such as the server address.

③ Enter the required information.

○ Your Mac jumps to the chosen location.

Save time with KEYBOARD SHORTCUTS

DIFFICULTY LEVEL

Most Macintosh owners do not realize that Panther makes it easy to change the global keyboard shortcuts, which work the same in all applications, for all sorts of operating system commands and applications. You may want to change a specific default because you find it hard to remember or difficult to use — or you may decide to add an entirely new keyboard shortcut for your needs.

Customize It ※

To add a new keyboard shortcut, click the + button in the Keyboard & Mouse pane of System Preferences. Choose the target application that will recognize the new shortcut and type the menu command that will be triggered by the shortcut. Note that the command name must be spelled exactly as it appears in the menu. Click in the Keyboard Shortcut box and type the new shortcut; then click Add.

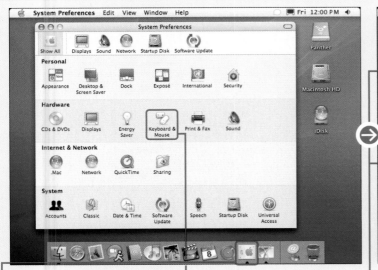

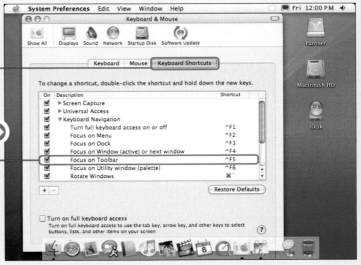

① Click the System Preferences icon in the dock.

○ The System Preferences window appears.

② Click Keyboard & Mouse.

③ Click Keyboard Shortcuts.

④ Double-click the shortcut that you want to change.

⑤ Press the new key shortcut.

⑥ Press ⌘+Q to quit System Preferences and save your changes.

Work automatically with CD AND DVD DISCS

#37

If you often listen to audio CDs or watch DVD movies, you can save yourself a few keystrokes each time that you load a disc: Set Panther to automatically launch your favorite application depending on the disc type.

The default applications are good choices — iTunes for audio CDs, iPhoto for picture CDs, and DVD Player for DVD movies — but you may specify other applications that you prefer instead.

Did You Know? ☀

If you load a blank recordable CD or DVD disc, Panther enables you to format that disc to accept files and folders from the Finder window.

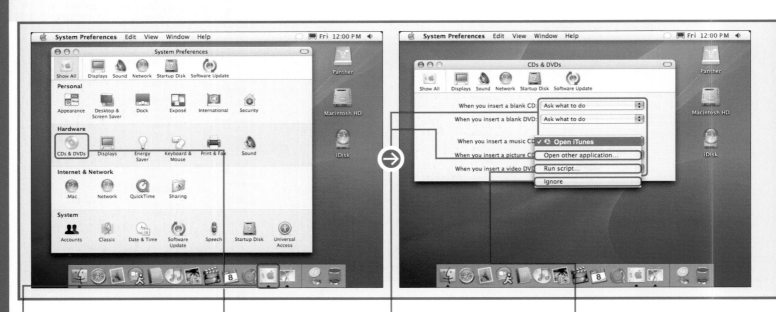

① Click the System Preferences icon in the dock.

○ The System Preferences window appears.

② Click CDs & DVDs.

○ The CDs & DVDs pane appears.

③ Click each drop-down list and choose the action for that type of disc.

○ Click Open Other Application to choose an alternative application.

○ Click Run Script to specify an AppleScript to be launched automatically.

○ Click Ignore to disable any automatic action.

④ Press ⌘+Q to quit System Preferences and save your changes.

Use Mac OS X SERVICES

DIFFICULTY LEVEL

Panther's Services menu enables you to streamline many common tasks — such as sending a file to a Bluetooth network device or creating a new sticky note with the contents of a file — without requiring you to launch the associated application.

Note that the services available for a specific file depend on the file's content and format. Some services are also available only when you have already selected a section of text or an image within a document or Web page.

Did You Know? ☀

Some third-party applications install their own commands in the Services menu, such as BBEdit and QuicKeys.

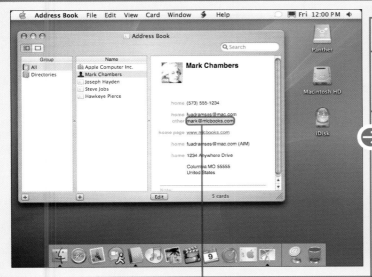

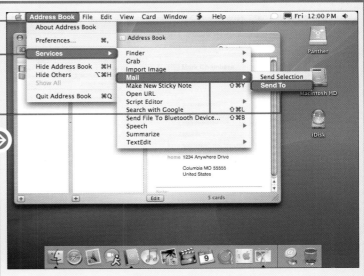

① Select a target file or folder in the Finder window.

○ Alternatively, you can select content from the active document, such as some text or an image.

② Click the application's named menu, such as Address Book.

③ Move your mouse cursor over Services.

④ Click the service that you want.

○ Panther launches the required application and prepares the selection according to the type of service.

⑤ Complete the task as you normally would have if you had launched the application yourself.

View files with
PREVIEW

Because Panther is so well connected to the Internet — and such a visual operating system to boot — it only makes sense that Apple would provide an image-viewing application such as Preview. Preview can handle an impressive number of different image formats, including both the familiar (JPG, GIF, and TIF) and the somewhat harder-to-find formats (PICT and PNG).

Panther also uses Preview to display PDF (Portable Document Format) documents, which are created by

Adobe's Acrobat application. These PDF files can be viewed on virtually all computer platforms in use today, including Windows, UNIX, and Linux. By using Preview, you can eliminate the guesswork about what application opens what type of image file; in fact, you can double-click directly on an image file, and Preview will automatically display it.

In this task, I demonstrate how to open and display an image file from within Preview.

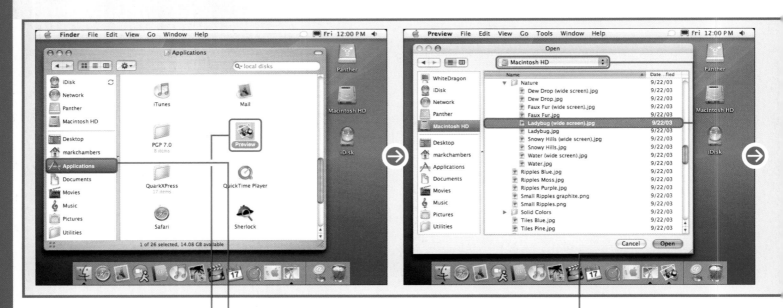

① Press ⌘+N.

○ A Finder window appears.

② Click the Applications folder in the Finder Places sidebar.

③ Double-click Preview.

Note: Preview does not launch with a window. You must open an image file before the Preview window appears.

④ Press ⌘+O to open an image file.

○ The File Open dialog box appears.

⑤ Navigate to the folder that contains the image file.

⑥ Double-click the file.

Did You Know? ※

Preview can convert an image
from one format to another; for
example, you can convert a TIF
image to a JPG image. To convert
an image, open it and click FileÍExport.
Type a new name for the file and click
the format that you want in the Format
drop-down list box; then click Save.

DIFFICULTY LEVEL

id You Know? ※

If you are viewing a PDF in Preview, you can
search for a specific string of characters. Open
the PDF in Preview and then press ⌘+F to display
the Search drawer. Type the text that you want to
find in the Search box, and Preview automatically
lists all occurrences of the text in the search list. To
highlight a specific occurrence in the document,
double-click its entry in the list.

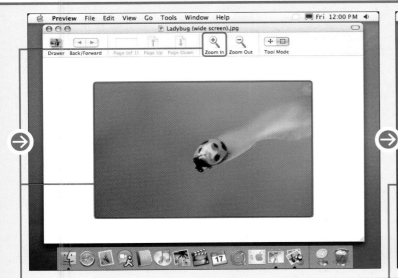

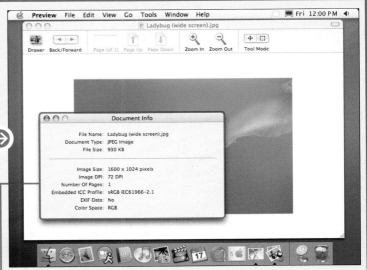

─○ Preview displays the
image.

⑦ Click Zoom In to magnify
the image.

⑧ Press ⌘+L to rotate the
image 90 degrees to the left
or ⌘+R to rotate it 90
degrees to the right.

⑨ To display information on
the image size, format, and
name, press ⌘+I.

⑩ Press ⌘+Q to exit
Preview and return to the
Panther desktop.

CHAPTER 4

Expanding Your Mac's Horizons

You are no longer a newcomer to Panther — you have mastered the basics of using the Finder, connecting to the Internet, launching applications, and manipulating windows.

Now it is time to raise the bar by moving on to some of the more advanced features within Mac OS X — tricks that can help keep you organized, protect your personal information, communicate with other devices, and even control your Mac with your voice. You may not need to use these features during each computing session, but they can really deliver in certain situations: For example, you may not have to create a PDF document every day, but when you need to offer a long document for downloading on your Web site, Panther's Save As PDF feature comes in very handy!

This chapter provides tips and tricks for experienced Mac OS X users. I demonstrate how to reveal the UNIX command prompt, how to enhance data security with FileVault and Secure Empty Trash, and how to boot from a specific operating system. This chapter also includes information on connecting with portable devices using iSync and shows you how to add new fonts to your system. For those who need a little organization help, I cover how to use Stickies to jot simple notes and how to add an event or appointment in iCal. Finally, I demonstrate Panther's powerful voice command feature, which activates an entirely new method of operating your computer.

TOP 100

#40   Connect to other devices
with iSync 60

#41   Use stickies on your desktop 61

#42   Access UNIX with Terminal. 62

#43   Delete your trash securely 63

#44   Protect your privacy with FileVault 64

#45   Start applications automatically when
you log in 65

#46   Activate voice commands 66

#47   Save documents as PDF files. 67

#48   Run multiple versions of Mac OS 68

#49   Configure your personal Address
Book card. 69

#50   Add a new font. 70

#51   Take screenshots with Grab. 71

#52   Add a new event in iCal 72

#53   Editing text files with
TextEdit 74

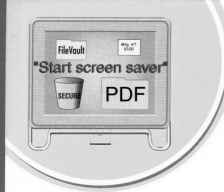

CONNECT
to other devices with
ISYNC

Panther's iSync application turns your Macintosh and your iPod into the best of friends — and you can expand this group by exchanging information between Mac OS X and many cellphones and PDA units.

A portable device must first be connected to your Mac — using a wired connection, such as USB or FireWire, or a wireless Bluetooth connection — before you can follow the steps in this task.

Did You Know? ※

After you have added a device, iSync will automatically recognize that device whenever you run the application. Of course, the device must be connected first.

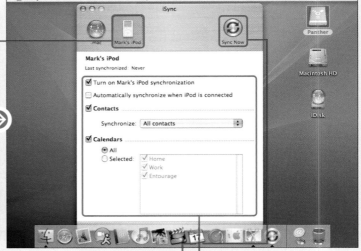

① Click Applications in the Finder Places sidebar.

② Double-click iSync.

  ○ The iSync window appears.

③ Press ⌘+N.

  ○ iSync displays the Add Device dialog box.

④ Double-click the device that you want to use.

  ○ The iSync window expands to show you what data can be synchronized.

⑤ Click the check boxes for the data that you want to exchange (☐ changes to ☑).

Note: For example, with my iPod connected, I can copy my Mac OS X Contacts and Calendar data.

⑥ Click Sync Now.

Use STICKIES
on your desktop

#41

Although the name is a little silly, Panther's Stickies application may save you from ever buying paper reminder notes again. Panther's stickies mimic paper sticky notes, enabling you to place multiple notes for yourself anywhere on your desktop. If you want to, you can place reminders all over your Mac OS X desktop, where they will be noticeable. Stickies windows can even be made translucent or assigned different colors to help you determine their priority.

Did You Know?

Stickies share many of the features of a text editor or word-processing application: You can print the contents of the active note, export text to a file on your hard drive, and even include graphics by dragging them into the note window.

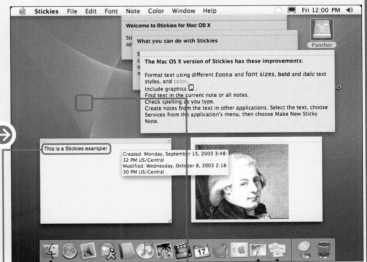

(1) Click Applications in the Finder.

(2) Double-click Stickies.

○ Your existing Stickies appear.

(3) To create a new Stickies note, press ⌘+N.

(4) Type the contents of the note.

Note: You can format your text with ⌘+B (bold), ⌘+I (italic), and ⌘+U (underline).

(5) To save all open stickies, press ⌘+S.

(6) When you have finished entering text, click any open area on your desktop to return to the Finder.

(7) To close Stickies, press ⌘+Q.

Access
UNIX WITH TERMINAL

42

DIFFICULTY LEVEL

Mac OS X is stable, reliable, and fast due to its UNIX foundation — but unless you use the Terminal application, you will never see the UNIX command line. If you want to type UNIX commands or you would like to handle an FTP session "the old-fashioned way," use Terminal to launch a UNIX command-line session.

When you first launch Terminal, your current directory is your Home folder — a convenient place to start if you want to edit a document.

Did You Know?

Mac OS X Panther ships with a complete collection of industrial-strength UNIX programs, including the Apache Web server, FTP, the Sendmail e-mail server, and the emacs text editor. If you are interested in learning how to use UNIX, start with Mac OS X . . . or a good UNIX book, such as *UNIX For Dummies,* 4th Edition, by John R. Levine and Margaret Levine Young (also from Wiley Publishing).

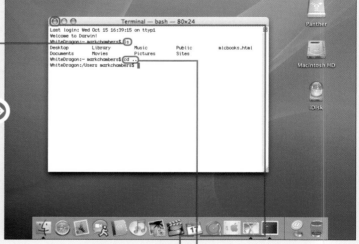

① Click Applications in the Finder.

② Double-click the Utilities folder.

③ Double-click Terminal.

○ The Terminal window appears.

④ To display the contents of the current directory, type **ls** and press Return.

⑤ To display help information for any command, type **man <command name>** and press Return.

⑥ To change to the parent directory of the current directory, type **cd ..** and press Return.

⑦ To quit Terminal, type **exit** and press Return; then click the Close button.

○ Terminal logs you out.

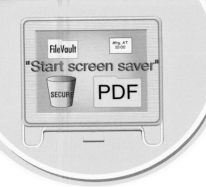

Delete your
TRASH
securely

DIFFICULTY LEVEL

When you empty your Trash by clicking Finder ⇨ Empty Trash or with the ⌘+Shift+Delete keyboard shortcut, you may think that the contents are gone forever; however, that is really not true. Those files can still be read using a third-party disk utility such as Norton SystemWorks, and the data can be restored.

If you are working with sensitive or personal data that needs to be erased — *permanently* — then use the Secure Empty Trash menu command, which overwrites the contents of the

Trash several times with random data and prevents those files from being restored in the future.

Did You Know? ※

Items that you have moved to the Trash remain there until you use one of the two Empty Trash commands. To restore a file from the Trash, simply double-click the Trash icon in the dock to display the contents and then drag the folder or file back to its original location.

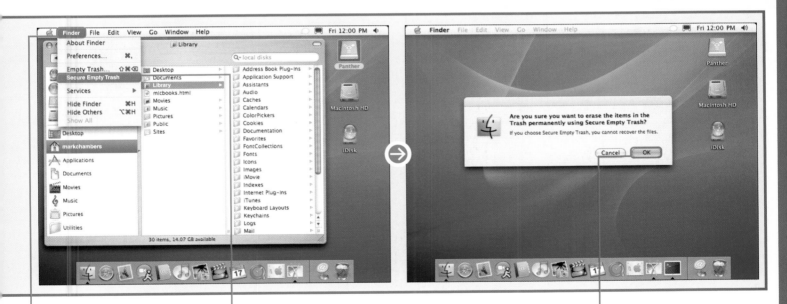

① Click Finder.

② Click Secure Empty Trash.

○ The Secure Empty Trash confirmation dialog box appears.

③ Click OK.

○ Your Trash is deleted securely.

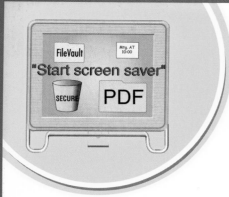

Protect your privacy with
FILEVAULT

If you are sharing your Macintosh with others, you may be concerned about securing the files in your Home folder against prying eyes. Panther has added a new feature called FileVault, which protects your Home folder by encrypting its contents.

Before you can turn on FileVault protection for your account, the FileVault master password must be set by an Admin-level user (see task #24 for more information).

Caution! ❋

Make sure that you have closed any open documents before you enable FileVault protection so that you do not lose any changes.

Caution! ❋

If you forget your login account password and an Admin-level user cannot provide the correct master password, the contents of your Home folder are lost *permanently*; the encryption cannot be removed without one of these passwords.

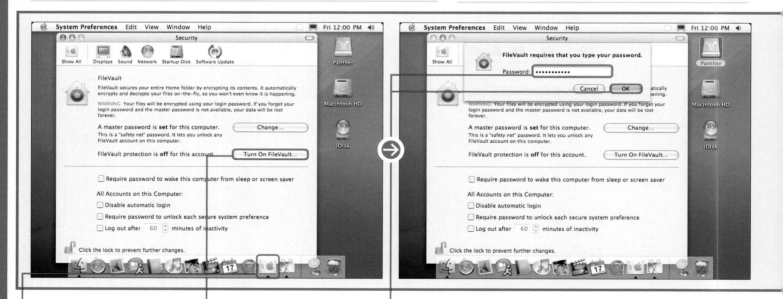

① Click the System Preferences icon in the dock.

○ The System Preferences window appears.

② Click Security.

○ The Security settings appear.

③ Click Turn On FileVault.

○ Panther displays a Password dialog box.

④ Type your account's login password.

⑤ Click OK.

○ Panther displays a confirmation dialog box.

⑥ Click Turn On FileVault.

○ Panther shuts down all running applications and displays an encryption progress dialog box.

⑦ Click your account in the login window and log in normally.

START APPLICATIONS AUTOMATICALLY

when you log in

Do you find yourself running the same set of applications each time that you log in? You can use Panther's Startup Items feature to automatically launch any number of applications as soon as you log in to Mac OS X. You can even specify the order in which the applications run. Note, however, that the current user can only modify the Startup items assigned to his or her account.

Did You Know?

You can allow a Startup item to run hidden in the background by enabling its Hide check box in the Startup Items list of the System Preferences Accounts pane.

Did You Know?

To remove an application from the Startup Items list of the System Preferences Accounts pane, select the application in the list and click the Remove button, which sports a minus sign.

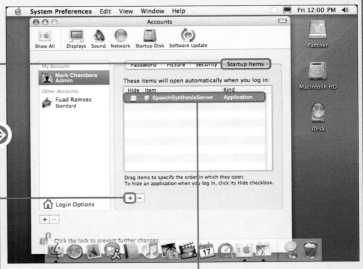

① Click the System Preferences icon in the dock.

○ The System Preferences window appears.

② Click Accounts.

○ The Accounts settings appear.

③ Click Startup Items.

④ Click the Add button.

○ Panther displays an Open dialog box.

⑤ Navigate to the location of the application that you want to start when you log in and double-click it.

○ The application is added to the Startup Items list.

⑥ Press ⌘+Q to quit System Preferences and save your changes.

Activate
VOICE COMMANDS

#46

DIFFICULTY LEVEL

With just a few clicks of the mouse, you can turn on the voice control system of your Mac, which comes as standard equipment with Panther. Your Mac can perform all sorts of chores via voice commands; although controlling your computer with your voice is not as precise as using your mouse and keyboard, I think that you will find that voice commands can help you use your Mac more efficiently.

Did You Know?

To view the default spoken commands that Panther will understand, click the Open Speakable Items Folder button on the Speech pane of System Preferences.

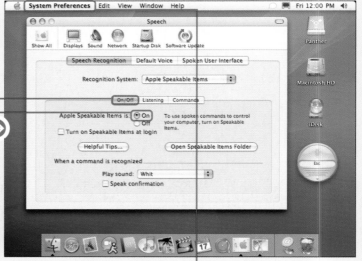

① Click the System Preferences icon in the dock.

○ The System Preferences window appears.

② Click Speech.

○ The Speech pane appears.

③ Click On/Off.

④ Click On (○ changes to ●).

○ The round Speech window appears.

⑤ Click Turn on Speakable Items at Login (☐ changes to ☑).

⑥ Click System Preferences.

⑦ Click Quit System Preferences.

○ You can now press Escape and speak a voice command.

Save documents as
PDF FILES

DIFFICULTY LEVEL

You do not need to install third-party applications such as Adobe Acrobat to create documents in the popular PDF (Portable Document Format) format. As long as you can print from an application, you can use the standard Print dialog box to produce PDF documents. PDF documents can be opened and viewed on-screen by any computer that can run Adobe's free Acrobat Reader (available at www.adobe.com), so they are great for distributing documents to users of different computer platforms, such as UNIX and Windows.

Did You Know?

You can use the settings of the Page Setup dialog box to adjust the orientation and scale of your document before you create a PDF document.

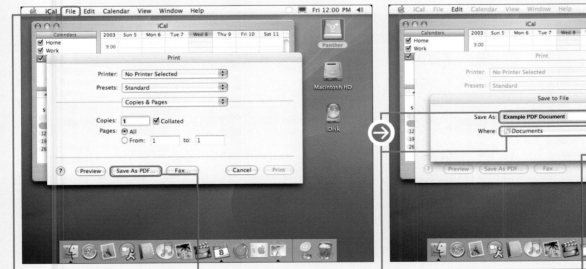

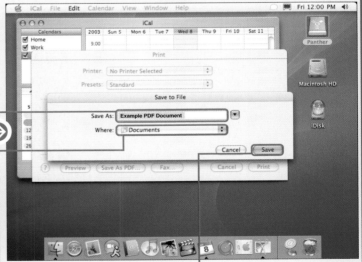

(1) Open the document that you want to make into a PDF.

(2) Click File.

(3) Click Print.

O Alternatively, you can press ⌘+P.

O The standard Print dialog box appears.

(4) Click Save As PDF.

O The Save to File dialog box appears.

(5) Type the filename.

(6) Click the Where drop-down list box and select the target location.

(7) Click Save.

O The document is saved as a PDF.

Run
MULTIPLE
VERSIONS
of Mac OS

Depending on the model of Macintosh you are using, Panther may be able to boot directly into Mac OS 9 — or, if you have more than one hard drive or a network connection, you may have access to bootable installations of different versions of Mac OS X. For example, I keep the current version of Mac OS X on one drive and the latest beta of the new version on my external FireWire drive.

You can switch between operating systems in System Preferences.

Caution! ☀

It is important to connect and power on any external drives before you open the Startup Disk pane of System Preferences; otherwise, the operating systems installed on those drives will not be displayed in the list.

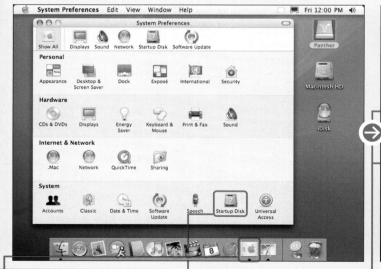

① Click the System Preferences icon in the dock.

○ The System Preferences window appears.

② Click Startup Disk.

○ The Startup Disk settings appear.

③ Click the bootable operating system to select it.

④ Click Restart.

○ Panther displays a confirmation dialog box.

⑤ Click Restart.

○ Your Mac restarts in the chosen operating system.

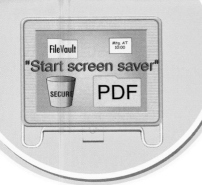

Configure your personal

ADDRESS BOOK CARD

#49

DIFFICULTY LEVEL

Panther's Address Book application stores one specific card for each user account that is tagged as the Personal record, or "My Card." The information on this card is used throughout Mac OS X by a number of different applications, including Mail and Panther's built-in faxing feature.

Customize It ☀

To change the picture that is used on your Address Book card, display your card and drag a new image file from a Finder window on top of the current picture. If the picture needs to be resized, Panther will show you what the new version will look like; drag the size slider to adjust the cropping. When the picture looks good, click Set. Remember, if you do not like the results, you can always click Cancel and try another image file.

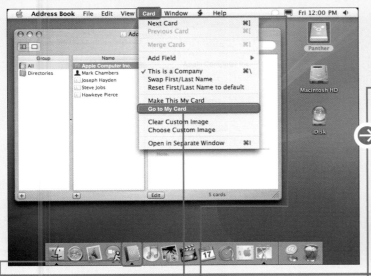

① Click the Address Book icon in the dock.

○ The Address Book window appears.

② Click Card.

③ Click Go to My Card.

○ Your personal card appears, denoted by the word "Me" next to the image.

④ Click in the fields and edit your personal data.

⑤ Press ⌘+Q to exit the Address Book and save your changes.

ADD
a new
FONT

DIFFICULTY LEVEL

Panther comes equipped with a new utility application called *Font Book,* which enables you to easily add and manage your collection of fonts. Because Mac OS X can recognize and use Windows TrueType fonts, you have a practically unlimited supply of commercial, freeware, and shareware fonts available — both online and at your local computer software store. Fonts that you add to your system through Font Book are automatically made available for your use throughout most of your applications.

Did You Know?

You can create new collections within Font Book that can help organize your fonts according to their theme. To do so, click the Add button, which bears a plus sign, and type the name; then drag fonts from the Font list and drop them into the new collection.

① Click Applications in the Finder.

② Double-click Font Book.

○ The Font Book window appears.

③ Drag the new font file into the Font list from any Finder window.

○ The font appears in the Preview box.

④ Press ⌘+Q to quit Font Book and save your changes.

Take
SCREENSHOTS WITH GRAB

DIFFICULTY LEVEL

Ever wish that you could capture the contents of an application window as an image file? With Panther's Grab utility, you can take snapshots of your Mac's display and save them to your hard drive in TIFF format.

Did You Know?

Besides a basic screen capture, you can also choose to capture just the active window or a selection that you can specify by dragging, which helps keep the size of the image file to a minimum. Choose Window from the Capture menu to include just the active window or click Selection to specify the area by dragging.

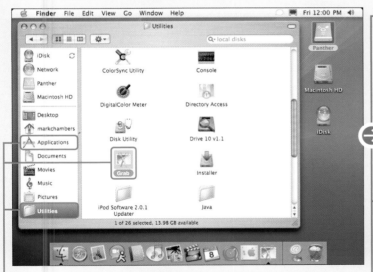

① Click Applications in the Finder.

② Double-click the Utilities folder.

③ Double-click Grab.

○ The Grab menu appears; Grab does not display a window when you first launch it.

④ Click Capture.

⑤ Click Screen.

○ The Screen Grab dialog box appears.

⑥ Click outside the Screen Grab dialog box.

○ Grab creates the image and opens it in a new window.

⑦ Press ⌘+S.

○ The Save dialog box appears.

⑧ Type a name for the screenshot and click Save.

○ The screenshot is saved.

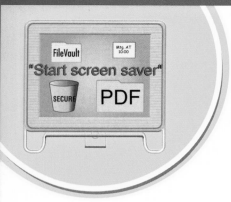

EVENT IN ICAL

Panther includes a great calendar and time management application called *iCal,* which you can use to track appointments and manage To Do items — complete with alarms and repeating schedules. In fact, if you subscribe to Apple's .Mac service, you can share your iCal calendars online with others and set up appointments based on the calendars that others share online. Within iCal, you can prioritize your events and To Do items to help you stay organized and, if necessary, create multiple calendars for home and office.

When iCal is combined with iSync (see Task 40), you will see that your events, appointments, and To Do items can be shared among all of your portable devices — which includes many mobile phones and PDAs, as well as your iPod and laptop. You can also save your iCal data to a disk file; exporting is useful for backups and trading calendars directly among friends and coworkers.

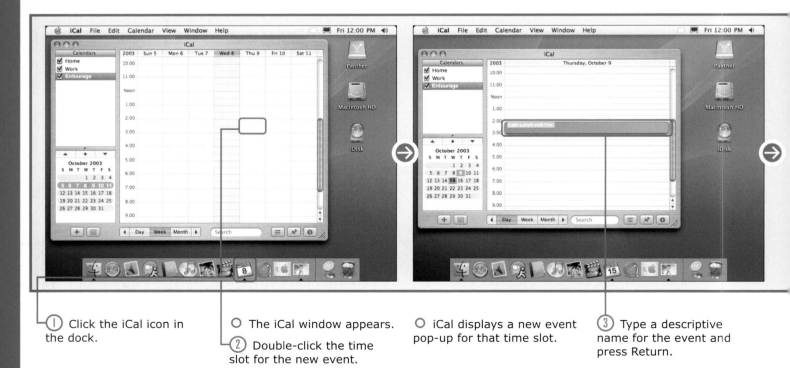

① Click the iCal icon in the dock.

○ The iCal window appears.

② Double-click the time slot for the new event.

○ iCal displays a new event pop-up for that time slot.

③ Type a descriptive name for the event and press Return.

Did You Know? ☀

It is always a good idea to keep a separate backup of your iCal data; in fact, I keep three backup copies, each a month apart. That way, I am able to access past appointments and events that I have recently deleted in my current iCal data. To export your iCal data to a disk file, click File ➪ Export and type a name in the Save As box; then click Export.

Did You Know? ☀

If you are currently using Microsoft's Entourage e-mail and calendar application, you can effortlessly import that data into iCal without retyping a single character. Just click File ➪ Import and then choose Import Entourage data from the Import dialog box. iCal will open Entourage and take care of the rest. Note that iCal can also import standard vCal data files from other applications.

④ Double-click the new event to edit it.

○ iCal opens the Editing drawer.

⑤ Click in the fields and enter information about the event.

○ iCal opens an editing box or displays a pop-up menu, depending on the field that you are editing.

⑥ Click the word *Notes* in the box to type a text note for this event.

⑦ Press ⌘+Q to quit iCal and save your new event.

TEXTEDIT

Mac owners commonly think of Microsoft Word or AppleWorks when they think of editing documents; however, these well-known applications are not always the best choice for a fast editing job on a file that includes only plain text. For example, you may need to edit an application configuration file or edit a text file that you have downloaded from the Internet.

When you need to make a change to a text file, turn to TextEdit, Panther's bare-bones text-editing

application. Do not be fooled by TextEdit's simple appearance: In fact, the application includes a number of advanced features, such as support for Rich Text Formatting (RTF) files, spell checking, justified paragraph formatting, and document styles.

In this task, I demonstrate how to open, edit, and save an existing text file on your hard drive.

① Press ⌘+N.

○ A Finder window appears.

② Click the Applications folder in the Finder Places sidebar.

③ Double-click TextEdit.

○ The TextEdit window appears.

④ Click File.

⑤ Click Open.

Customize It!

By default, TextEdit checks spelling as you type, underlining questionable words in red; however, if you find real-time spell checking distracting, you can choose to check your spelling manually. Click TextEdit ➪ Preferences and then click the Check Spelling As You Type check box to disable it. To check spelling manually at any time, press ⌘+; (semicolon).

DIFFICULTY LEVEL

Did You Know?

TextEdit can speak any text in the file — either the contents of the entire file or just the selected text. To speak text, click Edit ➪ Speech and then click Start Speaking. If you want to stop the spoken text, click Edit ➪ Speech and then click Stop Speaking.

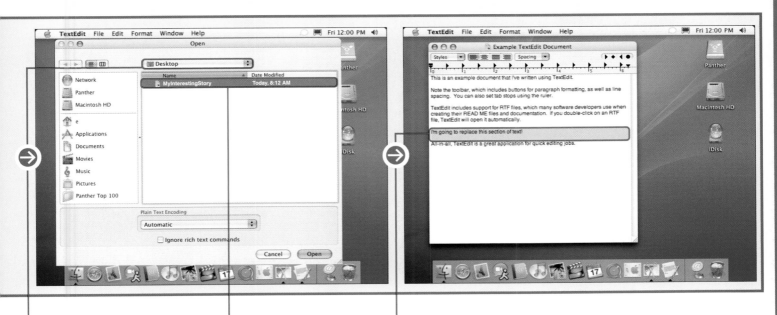

○ The File Open dialog box appears.

⑥ Navigate to the folder that contains the text file.

⑦ Double-click the text file.

○ TextEdit displays the contents of the file.

⑧ Click and drag to select the text that you want to change.

⑨ Type the new characters.

○ TextEdit replaces the selected characters with the text that you type.

⑩ To save the updated file, press ⌘+S.

⑪ Press ⌘+Q to exit TextEdit and return to the Panther desktop.

CHAPTER 5

Working with Multimedia and the Digital Hub

With the return of Steve Jobs to Apple a few years ago, the Macintosh experience has changed in dramatic ways. Chief among these changes is the Mac's role as the "Digital Hub." The idea behind the Digital Hub is that your Mac serves as the centerpiece of your digital world. You can connect still and video cameras, music devices such as the iPod, and CD and DVD burners to your Mac, the Digital Hub. The Mac OS takes care of coordinating tasks between these different devices, interpreting the media that each uses and producing useful output.

To help you along in your pursuit of digital nirvana, Apple saw fit to provide Mac users with a suite of digital media applications that offer professional results with a beginner's learning curve. This suite consists of iTunes for your music, iPhoto for your photographs, iMovie for working with video content, and iDVD for creating DVDs that play in home and computer DVD players.

Not only do the Digital Hub applications work great alone, but they also work well together. Apple has gone to great lengths to make the applications interoperate. The result is that your media tasks are easier to perform, take less time, and give you better results. With the Digital Hub, you can combine multimedia from audio, photo, and video sources into professional-looking presentations that you can then burn onto CD and DVD.

TOP 100

#54   Get photos, movies, and
music onto your Mac 78

#55   Convert audio with iTunes 80

#56   Burn DVDs with iDVD 81

#57   Burn CDs and DVDs with iTunes 82

#58   Use iTunes audio in iMovie 84

#59   Use iPhoto images in iMovie 86

#60   Fade iMovie audio in and out 88

#61   Add or remove the Ken Burns Effect 90

#62   Export iMovies for use in the hub 92

#63   Export iPhoto images 94

#64   Use iTunes to crop and split files . . . 96

Get
PHOTOS, MOVIES, AND MUSIC
onto your Mac

You can quickly and easily transfer multimedia from your favorite device. Panther can transfer and manipulate your favorite image, video, and audio media from digital and video cameras, audio CDs, an iPod, and just about anywhere else you can find it.

You can transfer photographs from digital cameras directly into iPhoto. This gives you the opportunity to tweak the look of the photos, catalog and print them, or even send them to friends. You can also import images into iMovie for use in your own movies.

You can also import your favorite video content into iMovie. After import, you can manipulate the video in a variety ways by adding titles, mixing in background music, and even adding sophisticated professional-quality video effects.

Panther also includes a complete set of tools for importing and working with audio. You can import your favorite songs from CD and the Internet using iTunes, iMovie, and iDVD. After import, you can catalog and listen to the song in iTunes or mix it in as background music for your movies in iMovie and iDVD.

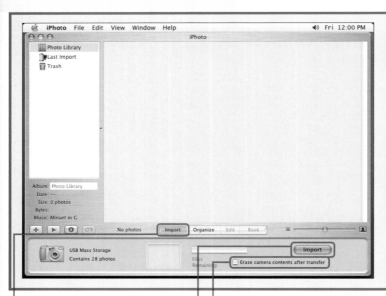

GET PHOTOS

① Launch iPhoto and click Import.

② Connect a digital camera to your Mac.

○ iPhoto displays a message when it is connected.

○ You can click Erase Camera Contents after Transfer to have the images on the camera erased after import.

③ Click Import.

○ iPhoto imports the images from the camera, adding them to the Photo Library.

GET VIDEO

① Launch iMovie.

Note: If asked by iMovie, choose to create a new project or open an existing one.

② Connect a FireWire video camera to your Mac.

③ Click the Camera switch to activate camera mode.

④ Click the Play button to begin viewing content on the camera.

⑤ When you see video that you would like to capture, click Import.

DIFFICULTY LEVEL

Customize It ※

You can listen to music in iTunes as you import it. Use the Preferences window to activate — or deactivate, if you prefer — the Play Songs While Importing setting. You can also set the default import format in the Preferences window under Importing.

Caution! ※

If you choose to erase the images from your digital camera when the import process in iPhoto is complete, be forewarned that you cannot reverse this procedure. After you erase the images from the camera, there is no way to regain them. Use this feature with care!

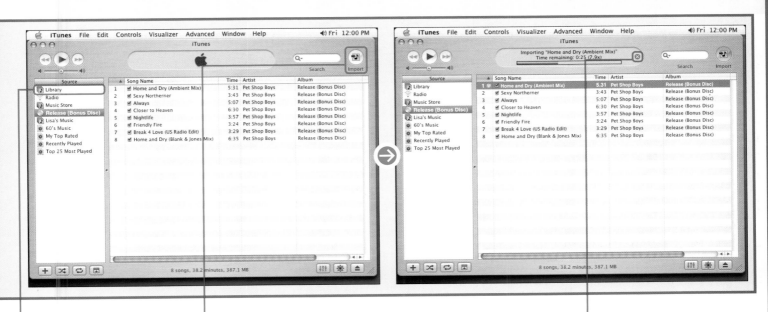

GET MUSIC

① Launch iTunes.

② Click Library to view the contents of the library.

③ Insert an audio CD into your Mac.

○ The names of the tracks on the CD appear in the iTunes window.

④ Click Import to add the tracks from the CD to your iTunes Library.

○ The music tracks are imported.

○ If you change your mind during the import, you can click X to cancel the import operation.

CONVERT AUDIO
with iTunes

DIFFICULTY LEVEL

You can convert audio for many purposes with the import tools built into iTunes — whether you are preparing audio for use on an audio CD or as Web content for a Web page.

Audio CDs require audio files to be in a particular format — AIFF or WAV. If you have files that are not in this format and want to include them on an audio CD, you need to convert them to AIFF or WAV. You can convert the audio when you import it or let iTunes take care of the conversion for you when you burn the CD.

You can also convert audio to the MP3 and AAC formats upon import. These file formats offer good audio content with smaller file sizes than AIFF and WAV. MP3 preceded AAC, so it is more universal. AAC provides a better-sounding file that is smaller than MP3, but you may not notice the difference. If you are importing audio for your personal playlists, go with AAC. If you are importing to trade with friends, use MP3. Your friends are more likely to have a computer that recognizes MP3 than AAC, although this gap is narrowing.

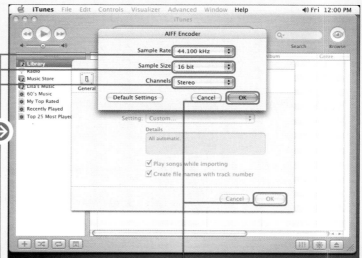

① Launch iTunes.

② Click iTunes.

③ Click Preferences.

○ The Preferences window appears.

④ Click Importing.

⑤ Select AIFF Encoder from the Import Using drop-down list.

⑥ Select Custom from the Setting drop-down list.

○ The AIFF Encoder dialog box appears.

⑦ Select 44.100 kHz from the Sample Rate drop-down list.

⑧ Select 16 bit from the Sample Size drop-down list.

⑨ Select Stereo from the Channels drop-down list.

Note: These are the settings for audio CDs. If you set Sample Rate, Sample Size, and Channels to Auto, iTunes sets the appropriate format.

⑩ Click OK and then click OK again in the Preferences window.

BURN DVDS
with iDVD

DIFFICULTY LEVEL

With the iDVD application, you can create and burn DVDs. Burning a DVD is the absolute last step in the DVD creation process, so make sure that you are finished before committing your work to a DVD. Furthermore, DVD-R discs are currently all that is available for Macintosh computers. The *R* means that you cannot erase the disc after you have burned it. If you make a mistake, you have just created a new coaster, and you will have to repeat the process after you make the necessary changes.

Did You Know? ☀

You can create a slideshow in iDVD directly from iPhoto. Launch iPhoto, choose a photo album, and click the Organize button followed by the iDVD button below it. The photo album appears as a slideshow in iDVD.

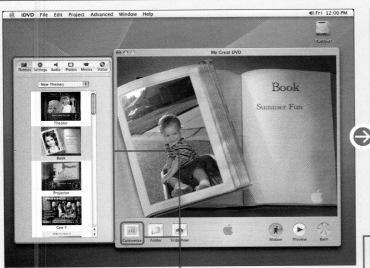

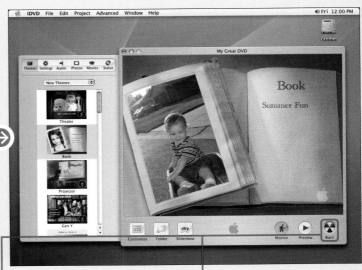

① Launch iDVD.

② Add video and photo content to the DVD by dragging it from the Finder and dropping it in the iDVD interface.

③ Click Customize to open the Customize drawer.

④ Adjust the settings for the DVD.

Note: In the drawer, set the theme, background image, font size, background music, and button style for the DVD.

⑤ Click Burn.

Note: This tells iDVD that you are ready to begin the DVD burning process.

⑥ Click Burn again to commence the burning.

○ iDVD prompts you to insert a blank DVD-R disc.

BURN CDS AND DVDS
with iTunes

You can use iTunes to burn your music onto CDs and DVDs in a variety of popular formats. The iTunes Preferences window gives you several options for burning discs. You can select the drive with which you want to burn, how fast you want the burner to operate, and the format of the resulting burned disc.

You have three format choices for burning discs in iTunes — Audio, MP3, and Data. Audio CDs are the discs that you will find in your home stereo, boom

box, or car. MP3 discs work in some CD players, some DVD players, and nearly all computers, such as your Microsoft Windows brethren. Data discs are only readable with a computer. Note that the Data format permits the burn to occur on a DVD disc as well as a CD. Using a DVD is a great way to back up large libraries. Choose the appropriate format according to your specific needs.

 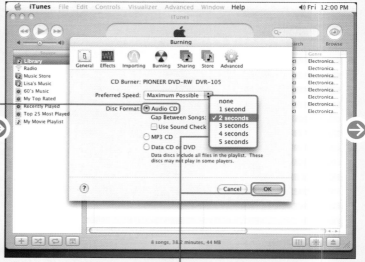

① Launch iTunes.

② Click iTunes.

③ Click Preferences.

○ The iTunes Preferences window appears.

④ Click Burning.

⑤ Click Audio CD to create an audio CD (○ changes to ●).

○ You can click the Gap Between Songs drop-down list and set the amount of silence that you want between each track on the audio CD.

⑥ Click OK.

#57

DIFFICULTY LEVEL

Apply It ※

If you want to burn additional discs that are identical to one you have already burned, select the playlist and click Burn Disc again. You can make as many copies as you want with one exception: The songs you download from the iTunes Music Store have limits as to how many times you may make copies. The number is large for individual use but is meant to prevent large-scale piracy.

Caution! ※

If you are using CD-R media, make sure that you have your playlist set exactly as you want it. If you make a mistake, you will waste a CD-R. CD-RW discs, on the other hand, are erasable, which gives you more room for error. CD-RW discs cannot, however, make up for the lost time of burning another disc when you make a mistake.

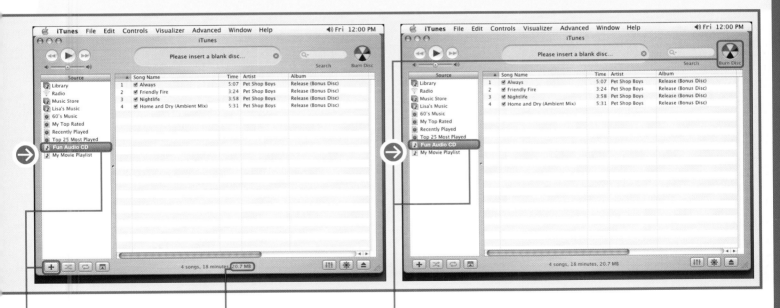

⑦ Click + to create a new playlist.

⑧ Name the playlist in the Source list.

⑨ Drag songs from the library to the playlist.

○ As you add items, the size of all the files appears here.

Note: Do not forget that most CD-R(W) discs have a capacity between 650MB and 700MB.

⑩ Click the playlist to select it.

⑪ Click Burn Disc.

○ iTunes prompts you to insert a blank disc if one is not inserted already.

○ The disc begins to burn.

Use iTunes
AUDIO IN IMOVIE

You can use audio that you have imported into iTunes with your iMovie creations. This helps you keep audio files organized with iTunes's excellent playlists while maintaining one-click access to that content in iMovie where you can use it.

You can use audio from iTunes to add background music for romantic movies, sound effects for action clips, and voice-overs for documentaries. When you add iTunes audio to an iMovie, iMovie imports a copy

of the audio, which becomes part of the current iMovie project. By importing the audio into your iMovie project, you keep the original iTunes audio unaltered for future use.

In iMovie, you can preview the audio, adjust its volume, use it in a movie clip, and even fade it in and out. Again, the changes that you make to the audio in an iMovie project do not affect the original audio in iTunes.

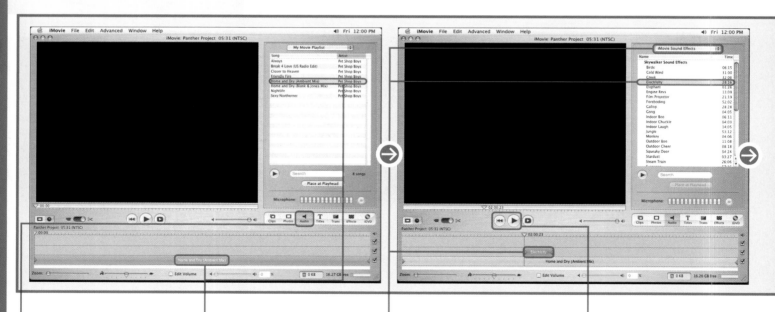

① Launch iMovie.

② Click Audio to reveal the audio tray.

○ Your iTunes Library and playlists appear in the audio tray.

③ Choose a song from one of your playlists that you would like to use in a movie.

④ Drag that song from the audio tray to the last track in the Timeline.

⑤ Choose iMovie Sound Effects from the drop-down list at the top of the audio tray.

⑥ Drag a sound effect from the audio tray to the second audio track in the Timeline.

○ If you rewind the movie and click the Play button, iMovie mixes the two audio tracks together upon playback.

Customize It ※

Not only can you overlap sounds in two different audio tracks, but you can even do so in the same audio track. If you drag one audio clip on top of another, the two clips will play back mixed together.

Did You Know? ※

You can create simple echo effects in your movie by layering multiple copies of the same audio clip. To make the audio echo, move each clip to a position that is slightly later in the Timeline than its preceding clip. To really mimic an echo effect, you can also adjust the volume of each clip, with each sound becoming quieter as you move down the Timeline. The clips that form the echo can appear in the same track or in different tracks.

DIFFICULTY LEVEL

⑦ Click and drag the sound effect and place it somewhere earlier in the Timeline.

⑧ Click the Play button.

○ iMovie instantly remixes the audio tracks, accounting for any changes that you made.

⑨ Click the sound effect that you added to the track.

⑩ Click Edit ➭ Copy to copy the sound effect to the clipboard.

⑪ Click Edit ➭ Paste.

○ When you paste the sound effect, iMovie creates a copy of the audio snippet in the same track, immediately following the sound effect that you copied. This is handy for duplicating a sound quickly.

Use IPHOTO IMAGES IN IMOVIE

You can use images that you have imported with iPhoto in your iMovies. You can take advantage of the organization that iPhoto affords you and maintain one-click access to iPhoto images in iMovie, in which you can use the images as part of a movie.

You can use images from iPhoto to create title screens, background images, or photo-movie slideshows. When you add iPhoto images to an iMovie, iMovie imports a copy of the image, which

in turn becomes part of the current iMovie project. By importing the images into your iMovie project, you keep the original iPhoto images unchanged for other uses.

In iMovie, you can zoom in on an image, place it in the frame wherever you want, and apply motion effects to it. The changes that you make to an image in an iMovie project do not affect the original image in the iPhoto Library.

① Launch iPhoto.

② Import a photo from a digital camera.

Note: See task #54 for more information.

○ iPhoto adds the photo to the Photo Library.

③ Choose the newly imported photo from the Photo Library.

④ Click Edit.

○ You can adjust the brightness, contrast, red-eye reduction, and other aspects of the photo.

Did You Know? ※

When you customize images in iPhoto, you must reimport them into your iMovie project for the changes to appear in your movie.

Caution! ※

When preparing images for use with iMovie, keep in mind that they should maintain a size ratio of 4 x 3, with 768 x 576 being the minimum dimensions. If you use an image that does not conform to a 4 x 3 ratio, iMovie may crop the image to conform to 4 x 3. This can result in less-than-optimal-looking results. Use a graphics application such as Adobe Photoshop to resize the image to the appropriate size.

⑤ Launch iMovie.

⑥ Click Photos to reveal the photos tray.

○ Your iPhoto Photo Library and photo albums appear in the photos tray.

⑦ Choose a photo from one of your photo albums that you would like to use in a movie.

⑧ Drag that photo from the photos tray to the topmost track in the Timeline.

⑨ Drag the image in the Preview window to reposition it in the scene.

⑩ Adjust the Duration and Zoom sliders to your liking.

⑪ Click Update to apply the changes that you made to the photo.

FADE IMOVIE AUDIO
in and out

You can fade iMovie audio in and out over time. The iMovie interface has a convenient Timeline in which you arrange audio clips in the order that they will play during the movie. You can adjust the volume of the audio in the Timeline over time.

To create a fade, you first place two markers on the volume-level bar in the Timeline. You adjust the volume of the second marker in relation to the first marker, making its volume lower.

Fading is useful for a multitude of tricks. Using two audio tracks — one with music and the other with speech — you can fade music to a lower volume when someone speaks. After the speech is completed, fade the music back in at a higher volume. You can also use fades to create audio effects that were not part of the original clip. As someone walks closer to the camera in a clip, for example, you could slowly increase the volume of the footsteps in the audio track. You will be surprised at how professional the results seem when you use tricks such as these.

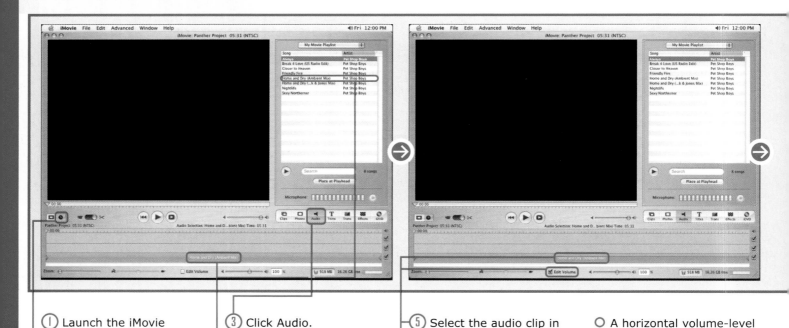

① Launch the iMovie application.

② Click the Timeline Viewer button.

○ The separate tracks appear in the Timeline at the bottom of the interface.

③ Click Audio.

○ The audio tray opens.

④ Drag an audio clip from the audio tray to the Timeline Viewer.

○ A colored bar appears indicating the length and location of the audio clip in the movie.

⑤ Select the audio clip in the Timeline.

⑥ Click Edit Volume (☐ changes to ☑).

○ A horizontal volume-level line appears in the audio clip.

Customize It

You can continue adding handles throughout the track to adjust its volume in time. Move the playback head to synchronize the audio with action that the viewer sees.

DIFFICULTY LEVEL

Did You Know?

To delete a handle, simply select it and press Delete. As you drag a handle horizontally, it will cause other handles to disappear in its wake. If you accidentally delete a handle that you did not want to eliminate, you can get it back. Press ⌘+Z to undo your action. The handle reappears with its curves intact. You can even undo multiple mistakes. If you inadvertently erase three handles, for example, press ⌘+Z three times to reinstate them in the Timeline.

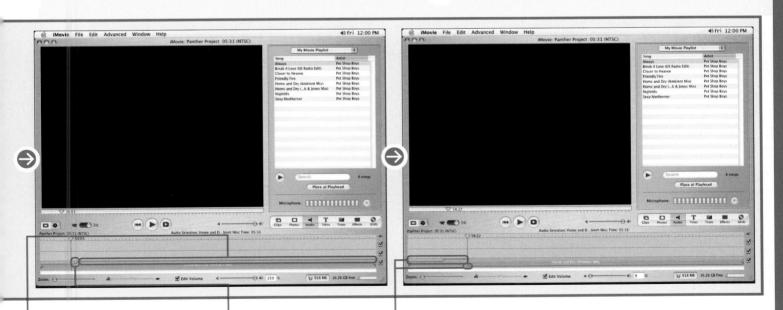

⑦ Click the horizontal line to add a handle to the audio clip.

○ A small circle appears on the horizontal volume-level bar.

⑧ Drag the newly added handle toward the top of the volume-level bar.

○ The volume increases at that point in the audio clip.

⑨ Click the horizontal line and add another handle to the right side of the previous handle in the audio clip.

⑩ Drag the handle toward the bottom of the volume-level bar.

○ The volume decreases from the level of the first handle to the level of the second handle, fading the audio out upon playback.

Add or remove the
KEN BURNS EFFECT

When you work with photographs in iMovie, you can apply the famous "Ken Burns Effect" to an image. This effect adds motion to otherwise lifeless still images. Used sparingly, the Ken Burns Effect can help you to create dramatic iMovie clips with just a few still images. If you use it too often, however, your movies can take on a gimmicky, if not seasick, feel to them.

Ken Burns is a world-renowned filmmaker. He is particularly known for creating documentaries. One of his signature styles is an effect whereby he positions a still photograph in front of a movie camera. He

then slowly moves the camera past the image, while zooming in or out on the photograph. This instills a unique feel to the photograph when viewed as a movie. You have, no doubt, encountered this effect in many television programs and movies. When you know what it looks like, you will find it popping up everywhere. The Ken Burns Effect simulates this fancy camera work digitally.

Although the Ken Burns Effect can make your photographs fun to watch, remember that a little goes a long way.

ADD THE KEN BURNS EFFECT

① Click Photos in iMovie.

○ The photos tray appears.

② Drag a photo from the photos tray to the Timeline.

③ Click the new clip in the Timeline to select it.

④ Click Start (○ changes to ◉).

⑤ Adjust the speed and scale parameters for the starting image.

⑥ Click Finish (○ changes to ◉).

⑦ Adjust the speed and scale parameters for the ending image.

⑧ Click Update to add the Ken Burns Effect to the photo clip.

#61

DIFFICULTY LEVEL

Apply It ☀

You do not have to use the Ken Burns Effect only for the standard effect that he uses. For example, you may remember scenes in movies that slowly pan starting at someone's feet to their head to indicate that they are very large or tall. You can accomplish this feat with the Ken Burns effect, too.

Customize It ☀

You can use the Ken Burns Effect to simulate the ground shaking. To do so, move the image upwards a small amount in the Preview window and set the speed for a very quick transition. Add the clip to the Timeline. Repeat the same effect in the reverse direction and add the clip to the Timeline. The quick up and down oscillations produce a believable ground movement.

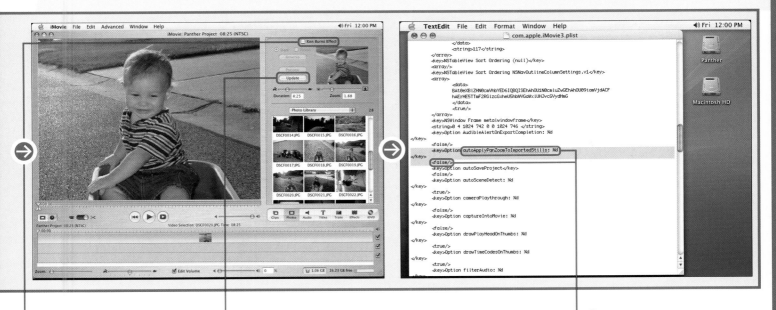

REMOVE THE KEN BURNS EFFECT

⑨ Click Ken Burns Effect (☑ changes to ☐).

⑩ Click Update.

○ The Ken Burns Effect is removed from the picture clip.

DISABLE THE KEN BURNS EFFECT BY DEFAULT

⑪ Quit iMovie and launch TextEdit.

⑫ Open the iMovie Preferences file.

Note: This file is at ~/Library/Preferences/com.apple.iMovie3.plist, where ~ indicates your Home folder.

⑬ Scroll down to the autoApplyPanZoomToImportedStills key.

⑭ Change "true" to "false."

⑮ Save the Preferences file.

Note: The next time you open iMovie, you will see that the Ken Burns Effect is now inactive by default.

EXPORT IMOVIES
for use in the hub

You can export your completed iMovie content to one of three or four formats: By default, you can export to a video camera, to a QuickTime file, or to an iDVD-ready file. If you have Roxio Toast installed, you may also see a VCD option in the Export dialog box.

Camera export sends the completed movie to a connected video camera. You can then use the camera as an intermediary to transfer the movie to a VCR or other similar device.

Exporting to iDVD simply presets the export settings to use the DV format that is appropriate for iDVD and Apple's DVD Studio Pro. If you need finer control over these settings, you can accomplish the same thing by exporting to QuickTime and making the settings by hand.

QuickTime export gives you the chance to export your movie to a large variety of video formats, including DV, AVI, and MOV.

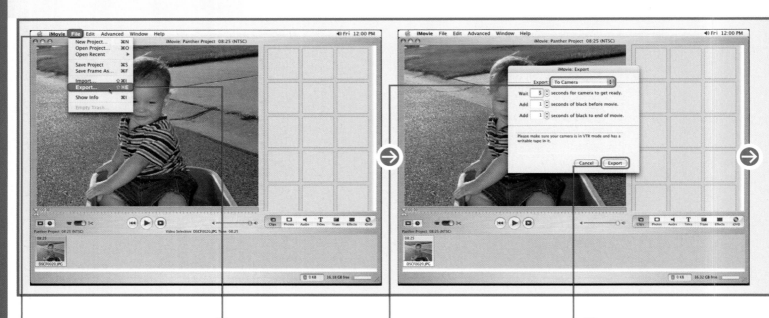

OPEN THE EXPORT DIALOG BOX

① In iMovie, click File.

② Click Export.

EXPORT TO A CAMERA

○ The Export dialog box appears.

③ Choose To Camera from the Export drop-down list.

④ Make sure that your camera is in VTR mode with a writable tape in it.

⑤ Click Export.

○ The movie is exported to the camera.

DIFFICULTY LEVEL

Customize It ※

iMovie makes life easier by offering you several preset QuickTime formats. If these formats do not meet your needs, choose Custom from the Formats drop-down list to manually select a QuickTime export format.

Did You Know? ※

If you are a registered QuickTime Pro user, you will see many more options under Formats in the Export dialog box than an unregistered user. To register for QuickTime Pro, open the QuickTime pane of System Preferences. Click Registration and enter your registration code. If you do not have a code, click Register Online in the registration window.

Caution! ※

Video files are large. In fact, sometime they are huge. Make sure that you have enough hard-drive space before you decide to make several copies of your movie in DV format.

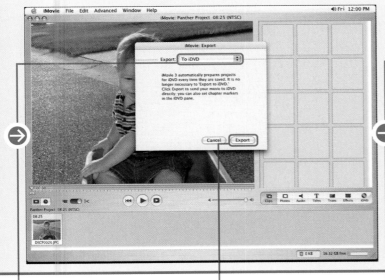

EXPORT TO IDVD

⑥ Choose To iDVD from the Export drop-down list.

⑦ Click Export.

○ The movie is exported directly to the iDVD application.

EXPORT TO QUICKTIME

⑧ Choose To QuickTime from the Export drop-down list.

⑨ Select a format from the Formats drop-down list.

Note: For example, you can choose Email.

⑩ Click Export to save the movie for the selected format.

EXPORT
iPhoto
IMAGES

The iPhoto application gives you many different options for exporting photographs to use in other applications. You can export an image or entire rolls of images.

You can use the File Export tab of the Export Photos dialog box to save images in JPG, PNG, and TIFF formats. JPG is useful for Web pages, e-mail attachments, and general-purpose uses where smaller file sizes are needed. PNG and TIFF files are much larger than JPG because they do not use compression. They also do not suffer from the degradation that JPG does.

You can export a roll of photographs as a set of Web pages by exporting via the Web Page tab, which offers settings that affect the HTML output of the export. You can upload this export to your Web site or store it on your hard drive for personal use in Safari.

The QuickTime tab permits you to save the image or roll as a QuickTime movie. This works well for creating a slideshow movie or when you need the QuickTime format for a still image in another application.

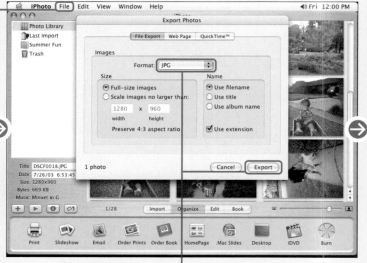

EXPORT AS A JPEG

① Launch iPhoto.

② Click Photo Library.

③ Click the photo that you would like to export from the Photo Library.

④ Click File.

⑤ Click Export.

○ The Export Photos dialog box appears.

⑥ Choose JPG from the Format drop-down list.

⑦ Click Export to export the image as a JPG.

Customize It ☀

The images that iPhoto uses do not necessarily have to be photographs. For example, you can create an image in a graphics application such as Adobe Photoshop and import it into iPhoto. This means that you can create a title page, text annotations, and other images, which you can in turn use as part of a QuickTime export in iPhoto. iPhoto is so versatile that you can even use it as a quick-and-dirty movie application.

DIFFICULTY LEVEL

Did You Know? ☀

Besides exporting images from an entire photo album, you can export individual photos as well. Select the images that you want to export by ⌘+clicking each one. Then export as normal. iPhoto exports only the selected photos.

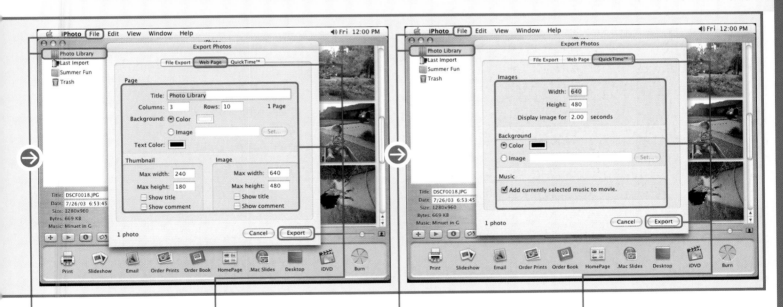

EXPORT AS WEB PAGES

8 Click to select a photo album in the Source list.

9 Click File.

10 Click Export.

○ The Export Photos dialog box appears.

11 Click Web Page.

12 Adjust the settings for your photo album Web pages.

13 Click Export.

○ iPhoto creates Web pages for your photo album, complete with preview images.

EXPORT TO QUICKTIME

14 Click to select a photo album in the Source list.

15 Click File.

16 Click Export.

○ The Export Photos dialog box appears.

17 Click QuickTime.

18 Adjust the settings.

19 Click Export.

○ iPhoto creates a QuickTime slideshow movie of the photos in your photo album, including subtle transitions between each image.

95

Use iTunes to
CROP AND SPLIT FILES

If you have an audio file that you would like to crop, you can use iTunes to perform the operation. It is not the most intuitive operation, but it is simple to use. This is handy when you want to remove extraneous sound at the beginning and end of an audio file. It is also useful for isolating a small snippet of sound from a file.

Using a similar set of operations, you can also separate a lengthy file into smaller chunks, each of which is a new audio file. This is great when you have extremely long audio files that you would like to split. This may happen, for example, when you record an LP record. It is easier to simply record an entire side of an album and then chop it up in iTunes later, rather than start and stop the recording process for each song on the album.

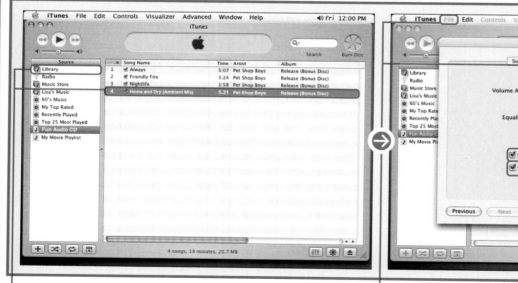

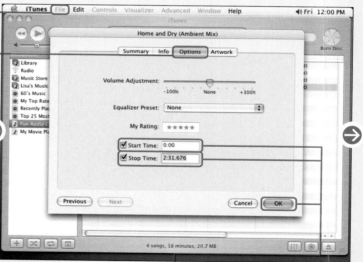

① Launch iTunes.

② Click Library.

③ Click a song in the library of which you would like to copy a segment.

④ Locate the exact times of where the clip to copy is.

Note: To locate where you would like the clip to start, move the playback head at the top of the iTunes interface. Write down that time. Then move the playback head to determine the end time of the segment.

⑤ Click File.

⑥ Get Info.

○ The Info window opens.

⑦ Click Options.

⑧ Click Start Time (☐ changes to ☑) and type the beginning time of the segment to copy.

⑨ Click Stop Time (☐ changes to ☑) and type the ending time of the segment to copy.

⑩ Click OK.

Did You Know? ※

When you extract a segment from an audio file in iTunes, iTunes gives the copy the same name as the original. It is probably a good idea to locate it as soon as you have finished creating it so that you can rename it. This may help prevent you from deleting the wrong file. If you are not sure which file is which, look at the time column of both tracks — the smaller one is the copy.

DIFFICULTY LEVEL

Apply It ※

After you complete the first conversion, you can continue separating audio segments from the file in a similar fashion. Select the start and end points as before and perform a new conversion for each segment that you would like to extract. Do not forget to rename the new file each time.

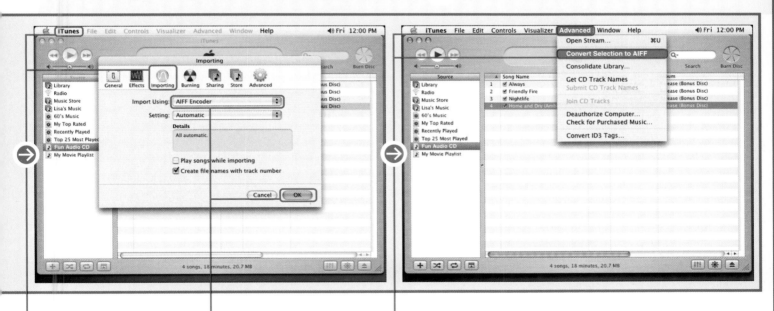

ⓘ Click iTunes.

ⓘ Click Preferences.

○ The iTunes Preferences dialog box appears.

ⓘ Click Importing.

ⓘ Click the format of the new clip.

Note: For example, you can choose AIFF Encoder.

ⓘ Click OK to apply the settings and dismiss the Preferences dialog box.

ⓘ Click Advanced.

ⓘ Click Convert Selection to AIFF.

○ iTunes converts the segment that you defined into a new track.

○ iTunes plays a "ding" sound when the conversion is complete.

CHAPTER 6

Troubleshooting Problems and Seeking Help

Sooner or later, even the most knowledgeable Mac power user encounters problems — and you will eventually need to troubleshoot Mac OS X Panther to determine what is wrong before you can fix it. *Troubleshooting* is an acquired skill that takes practice and logical deduction. Luckily, however, Panther is very reliable, so you should not have to troubleshoot often, and Apple provides you with tools that you can use to track down both hardware and software tribulations.

But what if you cannot fix what is broken? Even Apple tech support technicians are stumped from time to time. Therefore, it is important to know where to turn for help and

assistance in case you are stuck in the troubleshooting process.

In this chapter, I demonstrate how you can troubleshoot problems in Panther and how to locate additional help resources using Sherlock. These tasks introduce troubleshooting applications, such as the Disk Utility, Activity Monitor, and System Profiler, and discuss how you can use them to both monitor your system and fix many hardware and software errors. You will also find a number of Panther's more common features for dealing with problems: For example, this chapter covers how to update Mac OS X, force a misbehaving application to quit, and boot from a CD-ROM.

TOP 100

#65   Force a program to quit 100

#66   Use Mac OS X Help 101

#67   Fix hard drive problems with the Disk Utility 102

#68   Find out hardware and software information with the System Profiler 104

#69   Monitor your Mac's performance 105

#70   Search the AppleCare Knowledge Base 106

#71   Update Mac OS X 107

#72   Boot from a CD-ROM 108

#73   Uninstall applications the correct way 109

#74   Fix problems with user accounts 110

#75   Rebuild the Classic mode desktop 112

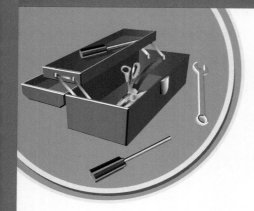

FORCE
a program to
QUIT

DIFFICULTY LEVEL

On rare occasions, an application may freeze or lock up, so you cannot use the familiar ⌘+Q shortcut to quit. For example, games are a prime candidate for lockups. A locked-up application may make you nervous — especially if you have important documents open in other applications — but rest easy! Panther keeps each application that you are running separate from other applications, so if a game crashes or your video-editing application locks up, you can terminate the misbehaving program without losing your other open documents.

Caution! ☀

Forcing an application to quit causes you to lose any unsaved changes you have made to the documents that application was using. **Always make sure that an application is definitely locked up (instead of just hard at work calculating something) before you force it to quit.**

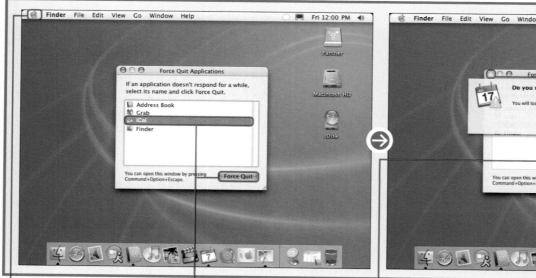 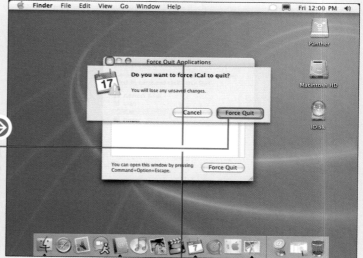

① Click 🍎.

② Click Force Quit.

○ The Force Quit Applications dialog box appears.

③ Click the application that you want to quit.

④ Click Force Quit.

○ Panther displays a confirmation dialog box to make sure that you want to force the application to quit.

⑤ Click Force Quit.

○ The application is forced to quit.

⑥ Click the Close button in the Force Quit Applications dialog box.

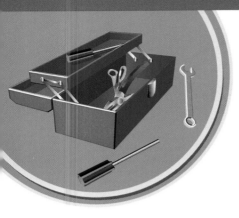

Use Mac OS X
HELP

#66

DIFFICULTY LEVEL

Panther includes a very extensive online Help system that you can search for specific keywords. Many Help topics include links that take you to other relevant Help topics, making it easier to narrow down your search to find the specific information that you need. You will also find that a number of topics enable you to open System Preferences panes or launch applications.

Did You Know? ※

Third-party applications can add their own Help topics to the Apple Help Viewer list, so as you install additional applications over time, you may find yourself locating more help information than you expected.

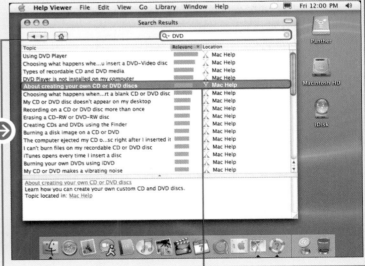

① Click Help on the Finder menu bar.

② Click Mac Help.

○ The Mac Help Viewer window appears.

③ Click in the Ask a Question box.

④ Type the word that you want to search for and press Return.

○ Mac OS X displays the Help topics that contain (or reference) your keyword.

⑤ Double-click a help topic in the list to display it.

⑥ When you have finished searching the Help system, press ⌘+Q to exit the Help Viewer.

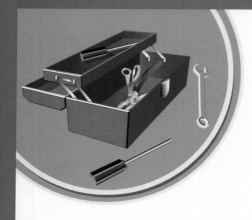

Fix hard drive problems
with the
DISK UTILITY

Hard drive errors can be caused by any number of events: a power loss, a misbehaving application, or physical damage caused by extreme heat or vibration. Mac OS X Panther includes a hard drive diagnostic program called the Disk Utility that can repair many types of errors that may crop up in your hard drive's folders and files. Of course, it cannot fix a hard drive with physical damage, but then again, no software utility can!

There are a number of third-party commercial disk utilities that perform much the same diagnostic and repair functions as Panther's Disk Utility; however, two applications — Drive 10 from Micromat at www.micromat.com and Norton Utilities at www. symantec.com — can both defragment your hard drive. Defragmenting can significantly improve the performance of your hard drive, so these utility applications make a good addition to the Disk Utility, which does not defragment your drive.

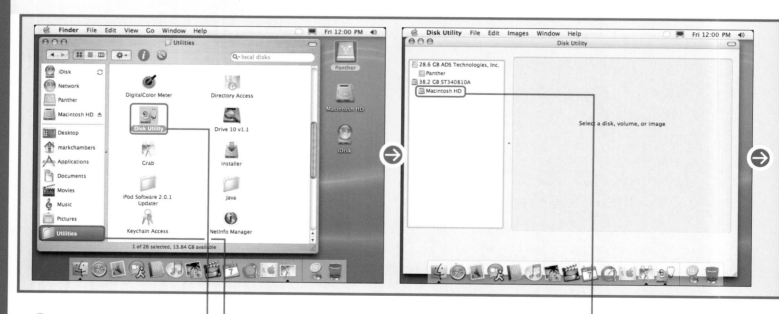

① Press ⌘+Shift+N.

○ A Finder window appears.

② Navigate to the Utilities folder, which is inside the Applications folder.

③ Double-click Disk Utility.

○ The Disk Utility window appears.

④ Click the hard drive that you want to verify or repair.

DIFFICULTY LEVEL

Did You Know? ✳

Mac OS X Panther
automatically and invisibly runs
the Disk Utility, verifying and
repairing the boot hard drive when you
turn on your Macintosh. This helps keep
your drive running smoothly behind the scenes.

Did You Know? ✳

You cannot verify or repair files on
your boot drive, which makes sense
because Panther is currently using it;
your boot drive is automatically verified
and repaired during the Mac OS X boot
process. However, if you are having problems
starting your Mac and Panther will not complete
the boot process, you can force Panther to boot
from the CD-ROM, enabling you to make repairs
to your boot drive: Load your Mac OS X installation
CD-ROM and turn off your Mac; then turn it back on
while holding down the C key.

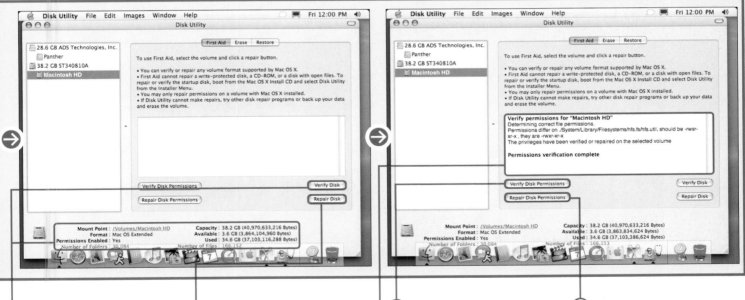

○ The Disk Utility displays
the statistics for the partition
and some buttons.

⑤ If the Verify Disk button
is enabled, you can click it to
verify the file structure of
the drive.

○ The Disk Utility displays
the result of the disk
verification.

⑥ If a problem is found
with your disk format, click
Repair Disk to fix it.

⑦ To verify the drive's file
permissions, click Verify
Disk Permissions.

○ The Disk Utility displays
the result of the
permissions verification.

⑧ If a problem is found
with your drive's disk
permissions, click Repair
Disk Permissions to fix it.

⑨ Press ⌘+Q to exit the
Disk Utility and return to the
Panther desktop.

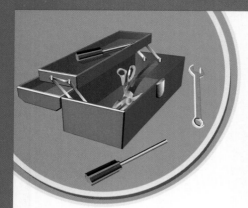

Find out hardware and software information with the SYSTEM PROFILER

DIFFICULTY LEVEL

What type of memory modules are currently installed in your Macintosh? What is the speed of your Mac's processor, and how many USB and FireWire ports are available? Do you know what applications you have installed and what their version numbers are?

You may need to find out the answers to these questions if you have to contact Apple's technical support or if you are trying to determine whether an application will run on your system.

Rather than disassemble your Macintosh or get dirty under your desk, you can answer these questions — and many more concerning your system's hardware and software — with the Mac OS X System Profiler.

Did You Know? ※

You can also use the System Profiler to display all the network connections and network settings currently operating on your Mac.

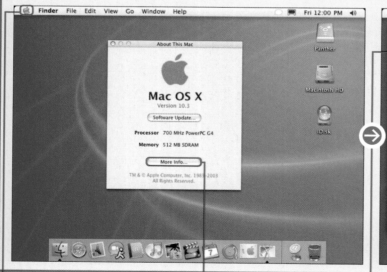

① Click .

② Click About This Mac.

○ The About This Mac dialog box appears.

③ Click More Info.

○ Panther launches the System Profiler.

④ Click the heading that you want to display in the Contents list.

Note: For a summary of your hardware or software, click Hardware or Software.

⑤ Click File ➪ Print to print the current contents of the Profiler window.

⑥ Press ⌘+Q to exit the Profiler.

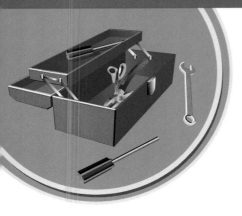

MONITOR
your Mac's
PERFORMANCE

 #69

DIFFICULTY LEVEL

When troubleshooting Panther or a Macintosh application, it is often helpful to monitor how much memory, processor time, and system resources are being used. Panther provides the Activity Monitor, a utility program that displays these figures, along with network and hard drive usage, in real time.

The Activity Monitor also enables you to view the processes being executed by Panther; a *process* is a discrete task (either visible or invisible) that Panther performs in order to run

your applications or to keep itself running.

Caution! ✳

Using the Activity Monitor, you can selectively delete a process. However, deleting a system process can result in **all** of Mac OS X locking up! Therefore, it is a good idea to delete a process only if instructed to do so by a support technician.

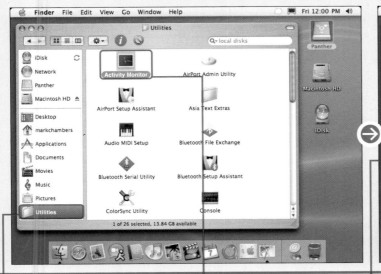

① Press ⌘+Shift+N.

○ A Finder window appears.

② Navigate to the Utilities folder, which is inside the Applications folder.

③ Double-click Activity Monitor.

○ The Activity Monitor window appears.

④ Click the type of information that you want.

Note: The Activity Monitor can display CPU usage, memory usage, disk activity and usage, and network activity.

⑤ Press ⌘+2 to display a CPU Usage window.

○ You can move this window anywhere on your desktop and monitor your CPU usage.

Note: Click Monitor ⇨ the dock icon to display different Activity Monitor information in the dock.

⑥ Click Activity Monitor ⇨ Quit.

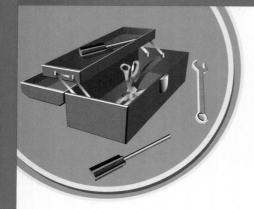

Search the AppleCare
KNOWLEDGE BASE

DIFFICULTY LEVEL

Although you may already consider Sherlock helpful in researching all sorts of things on the Internet — from the spelling of a word or the show times for a movie to flight schedules and driving directions (see task #86) — Panther power users know that Sherlock is also the perfect sleuth for delving into the AppleCare Knowledge Base.

The Knowledge Base provides you with the latest help from Apple technical support, including

solutions and workarounds to help you deal with specific hardware and software under Mac OS X.

Did You Know? ※

AppleCare and Sherlock make a great team, especially when you are searching for additional help with the text from an error or warning dialog box. Choose the phrase from the error message that is most likely to return a match.

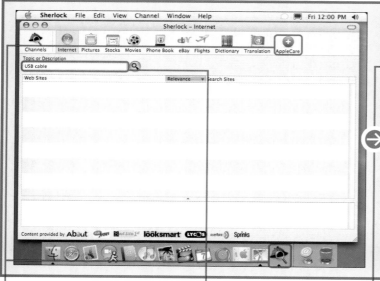

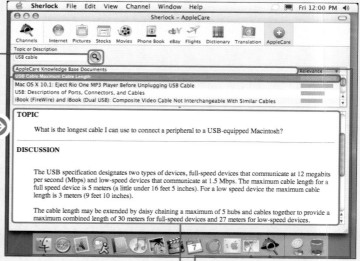

① Click the Sherlock icon in the dock.

○ The Sherlock window appears.

② Click AppleCare.

○ The AppleCare pane appears.

③ Type a keyword, topic, or part of an error message into the Topic or Description box.

Note: It is a good idea to limit your search text to four words or less, which will return more matches than a longer phrase.

④ Click the magnifying glass button.

○ Sherlock displays the Knowledge Base topics that match your target phrase, grouped according to likely relevance.

○ You can click AppleCare Knowledge Base Documents to sort alphabetically.

⑤ Click a topic.

○ Sherlock displays the topic's contents.

⑥ Press ⌘+Q to quit Sherlock.

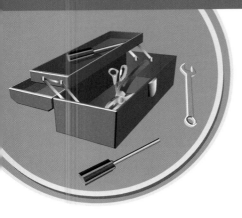

UPDATE
Mac OS X

DIFFICULTY LEVEL

Mac OS X may be both remarkably powerful and stable, but there is no such thing as the "perfect" operating system. Therefore, Apple has added an easy-to-use update system that you can use to install the latest bug fixes, operating system improvements, and Apple application updates.

You need an Internet connection to use Panther's update feature. The update process requires more time if you are using a dial-up modem instead of a broadband connection.

Customize It ※

You can set Panther to automatically check for updates behind the scenes on a schedule; check the Check for Updates check box and then click the time period drop-down list box to specify the schedule period. If you want Mac OS X to automatically download critical updates as well, check the Download Important Updates in the Background check box; note, however, that updates that are not regarded as critical must still be manually downloaded.

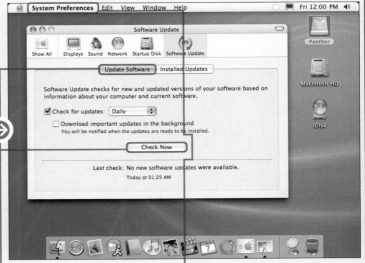

① Click the System Preferences icon in the dock.

○ The System Preferences dialog box appears.

② Click Software Update.

○ The Software Update pane appears.

③ Click Update Software.

④ Click Check Now to manually check for updates.

Note: If any updates appear, it is usually a good idea to install all of them.

⑤ Click the check box next to each update that you want to install.

⑥ Click Install.

Note: Some updates require that you restart your Mac and will prompt you to do so.

⑦ Click System Preferences ⇨ Quit System Preferences (if you did not have to restart).

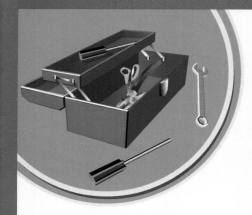

BOOT
from a
CD-ROM

What should you do if Panther itself locks up during the boot process? It is hard to troubleshoot Mac OS X if the operating system constantly freezes because of a system or hard drive error. Luckily, you are not limited to booting from your hard drive: In a pinch, you can actually boot Panther from your Mac OS X installation CD-ROM.

This trick also comes in handy when you want to boot from a third-party utility CD-ROM, such as Norton Utilities from Symantec (www.symantec.com) or DiskWarrior from Alsoft (www.alsoft.com).

Did You Know? ※

To display a system boot menu during startup — which acts much like the Startup Disk pane in System Preferences — hold down the Option key while starting or restarting your Mac.

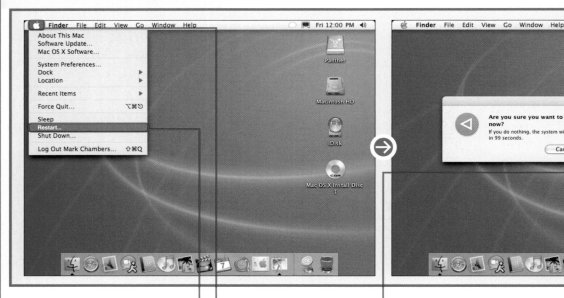

① Press the Media Eject key on your keyboard and load the CD-ROM from which you want to boot.

② Click .
③ Click Restart.

○ The Restart confirmation dialog box appears.

④ Click Restart.

⑤ Press and hold the C key on your keyboard.

⑥ Your Mac boots from the CD-ROM.

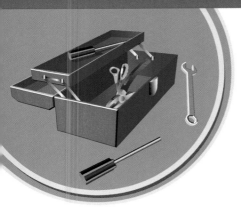

UNINSTALL APPLICATIONS
the correct way

DIFFICULTY LEVEL

Unlike Windows, Mac OS X does not include an Add/Remove Applications utility; most Macintosh developers follow the rule "One folder for each application." All the data files, and the application program itself, reside in a single folder, and usually all you need to do is delete that folder to uninstall the application.

There are exceptions — so follow the steps shown here each time you delete a Mac OS X application folder. Search for any Preference or data files that remain in other locations and delete them to save space on your hard drive.

Did You Know? ※

A number of shareware and commercial utilities can also perform the uninstall job; the best-known is probably Spring Cleaning from Aladdin Systems (www.aladdinsystems.com), which also removes Internet browser cache files and fixes broken aliases. The application even includes a Restore feature that can restore files that you have deleted by accident.

① Press ⌘+Shift+N.

○ A Finder window appears.

② Locate and delete the folder of the application that you want to uninstall.

③ Click in the Search box.

④ Type the name of the application that you just deleted.

*Note: For example, you might type **Photoshop** or **BBEdit**.*

○ Panther displays all filenames that include the target word.

⑤ Click a file.

⑥ If the file needs to be deleted, Control+click it.

Note: Generally, it is safe to delete an "orphan" file if it shares the same name and version number as the application you just deleted.

⑦ Click Move to Trash on the pop-up menu.

○ The file is removed from your system.

⑧ Repeat steps 5 to 7 for all the files with matching names and version numbers.

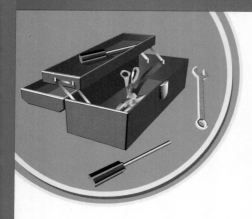

Fix problems with
USER ACCOUNTS

If more than one person is using your Macintosh — either from the local keyboard or across a network — then you have turned it into a multiuser powerhouse. Mac OS X does a great job of keeping personal documents secure and even maintains different desktop and application settings for each user that you create. Everyone's documents are kept separate and secure as well because each user has his or her own Home folder. A classroom Macintosh is a good example of a shared multiuser computer; each

student has an account, and the teacher uses the Admin account, the primary account created when you first set up Mac OS X.

However, if a person suddenly cannot log in or you have to tweak the capabilities of a user, you need to go troubleshooting in System Preferences; you can use the settings found on the Accounts pane. This procedure assumes that you are logging in as the Admin account.

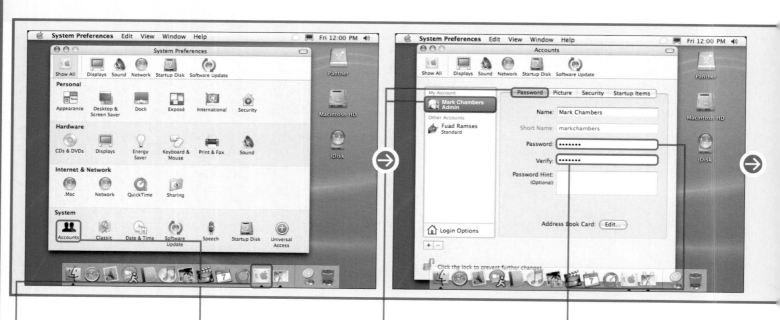

ACCESS ACCOUNT INFORMATION

① Click the System Preferences icon in the dock.

○ The System Preferences dialog box appears.

② Click Accounts.

○ The Accounts pane appears.

CHANGE PASSWORDS

③ Click the user account that you want to configure.

○ Panther displays the settings for that account.

④ Click Password.

Note: If the user tells you that his or her password is not working, you can reset it here.

⑤ Click in the Password field and type a new password.

⑥ Click in the Verify field and retype the same password.

#74

DIFFICULTY LEVEL

Caution! ※

Assigning a user an Admin account allows him to make changes within System Preferences and also allows him greater access to documents and applications within Panther: Therefore, **assign Admin privileges only to those who require higher access or experienced Mac OS X users whom you trust.**

Customize It! ※

If you no longer need to display the Login window and you will be the only one using your Macintosh, you can set it to automatically log you in. Click the Login Options button at the bottom of the Accounts list and click the Automatically Log In As check box to enable it; then choose your account from the drop-down list box. Do not forget to delete any old user accounts that you no longer need!

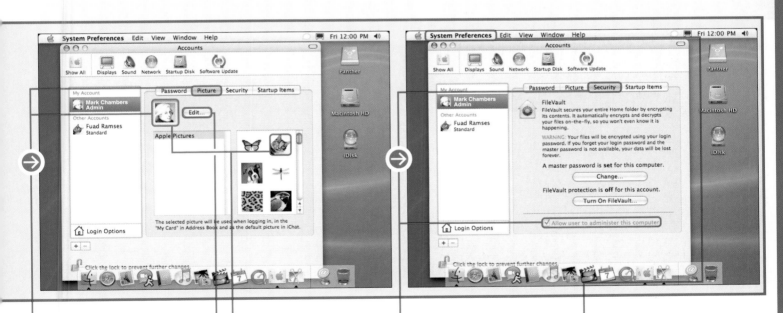

CHANGE A USER'S IMAGE

⑦ Click Picture.

Note: You can select a new thumbnail image for the account from this pane.

○ The image shown represents the selected user on the login screen and in iChat AV.

⑧ Drag an image thumbnail from the right column to the well.

⑨ Click Edit to add your own image.

Note: You can use a snapshot from your Mac's video camera or drag an image from a Finder window.

CHANGE A USER'S PRIVILEGES

⑩ Click Security.

⑪ Click Allow User to Administer This Computer to change the account security level (☐ changes to ☑).

Note: With this check box enabled, the selected user receives all Admin privileges.

⑫ Click System Preferences.

⑬ Click Quit System Preferences.

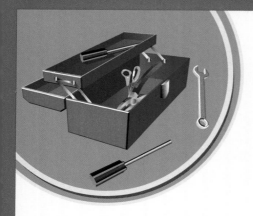

Rebuild the
CLASSIC MODE DESKTOP

Panther's Classic mode is the Great Pretender — do not be surprised to see the familiar Mac OS 9 Welcome screen appear on your Panther desktop! When you need to run an older application written before the days of Mac OS X, Panther automatically starts a special environment, called *Classic mode,* in which the application can run smoothly. In fact, the legacy application has no idea that it is actually running in Mac OS X, and you can continue to run your Mac OS X applications right alongside your Classic applications.

Like Mac OS 9 before it, however, your Classic mode desktop may sometimes require a database rebuild; this can solve a number of problems in Classic mode, including icons that no longer appear on the desktop and application document icons that no longer display correctly in the Finder window. The desktop database file may be corrupted by all sorts of events, including blackouts, misbehaving programs that lock up, and running out of hard drive space.

To rebuild the Classic desktop, you will need to run System Preferences and visit the Classic pane.

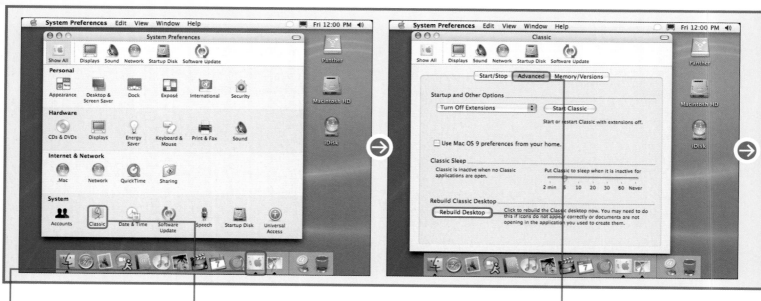

① Click the System Preferences icon in the dock.

○ The System Preferences dialog box appears.

② Click Classic.

○ The Classic pane appears.

③ Click Advanced.

④ Click Rebuild Desktop.

Did You Know? ☀

You can configure Classic to run automatically when you log in using the current account. Click the Start/Stop button and check Start Classic When You Log In. To completely hide the Classic launch progress bar, check Hide Classic While Starting.

Customize It! ☀

If you have multiple installations of Mac OS 9, remember that Panther enables you to choose which Mac OS 9 System folder is used to launch Classic mode. (This is handy if you need to load specific startup items or device drivers to use a certain Mac OS 9 application in Classic mode.) Click the Start/Stop button and then click the System folder that you want to use. By default, Panther uses the System folder on the same drive as your Mac OS X System folder.

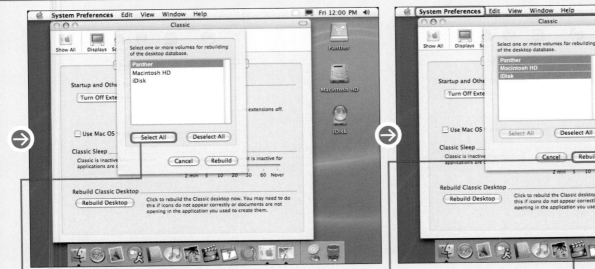

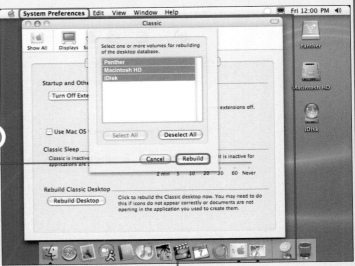

○ Panther displays the Volume Selection sheet.

⑤ Click Select All.

Note: Choosing Select All rebuilds the Classic desktop database using all the volume information from all the drives on your Mac.

⑥ Click Rebuild.

○ The Classic desktop database is rebuilt.

⑦ Click System Preferences.

⑧ Click Quit System Preferences.

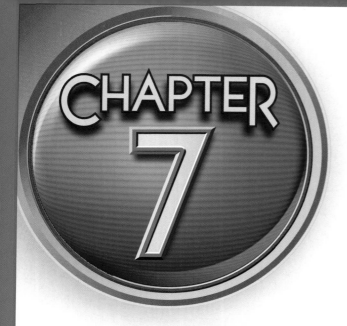

CHAPTER 7

Taking Advantage of the Internet

The Internet has become a major part of the personal computer landscape. Mac OS X has always provided great features to help you work on the Internet. Panther continues this tradition by updating some existing tools as well as adding new ones to the mix.

Safari, the Web browser included with Panther, just keeps getting better. With improvements in Safari, you can streamline your Web surfing, block pop-up windows, surf Web servers on your local network, and even view documents from your hard drive.

The Mail application continues to progress. With the inclusion of new antispam features and tight integration with other applications

such as the Address Book, Panther's e-mail can save you a lot of time.

Browsers and e-mail clients are not the only way to use the Internet in Panther. Sherlock is a great tool for finding specific information on the Web. With Sherlock, you can find what you need in a fraction of the time required using other methods, including searching for phone numbers, reading movie listings, and even tracking eBay auctions.

Panther makes it easy to run your own Apache Web server. With only one click, you can begin serving Web pages like the pros. With the power of Apache behind you, you will find that running a Web server has many benefits on your local network.

TOP 100

#76 Organize your Web surfing
with tabs...................... 116

#77 View and bookmark documents
in Safari 118

#78 Save Web pages on your hard drive 119

#79 Stop pop-up ads from appearing
in your browser................ 120

#80 Eliminate spam with Mail 121

#81 Manage threaded e-mail................. 122

#82 Set up a Web server 123

#83 Visit Web sites of people in your
Address Book 124

#84 Use Rendezvous to surf local Web sites...... 125

#85 Save Internet content for later use 126

#86 Use Sherlock to find information and
perform tasks 128

#87 Channel the power of the
Address Book in Mail......... 130

ORGANIZE
YOUR WEB SURFING
with tabs

You can organize your Web surfing and reduce clutter by using tabs in the Safari Web browser. Tabs enable you to open multiple Web sites within the same browser window. This prevents you from having to open multiple windows to accommodate multiple Web sites.

After you activate tabbed browsing in Safari, you can use tabs much as you would use the Open in New Window menu command in any other Web browser.

Each tab can display its own Web page. You can also open links in new tabs by using the tab keyboard shortcuts.

Each tab, like each window in nontabbed browsers, displays the title of the Web page within it. A tab also lets you know when it has completed the download of the Web page associated with it. Then, when you are finished reading the Web page shown within a tab, you can close it by clicking the tab's Close icon.

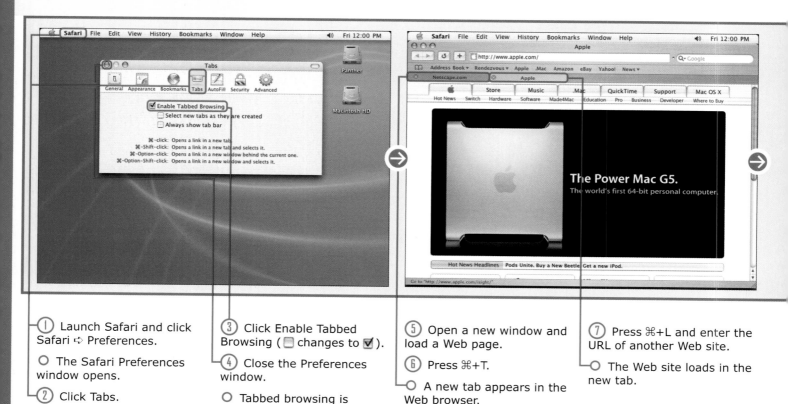

① Launch Safari and click Safari ⇨ Preferences.

○ The Safari Preferences window opens.

② Click Tabs.

○ The tab settings pane appears.

③ Click Enable Tabbed Browsing (☐ changes to ☑).

④ Close the Preferences window.

○ Tabbed browsing is now enabled.

⑤ Open a new window and load a Web page.

⑥ Press ⌘+T.

○ A new tab appears in the Web browser.

⑦ Press ⌘+L and enter the URL of another Web site.

○ The Web site loads in the new tab.

Did You Know? ※

You can quickly close all
the tabs in a Safari window by
pressing ⌘+Option+W. All tabs
immediately close, leaving the
enclosing window intact.

DIFFICULTY LEVEL

Customize It! ※

By Control+clicking a tab, you can access a
few hidden tab features. The contextual menu
that appears when you click permits you to reload
or close a specific tab. It also lets you close
all other tabs besides the current one.

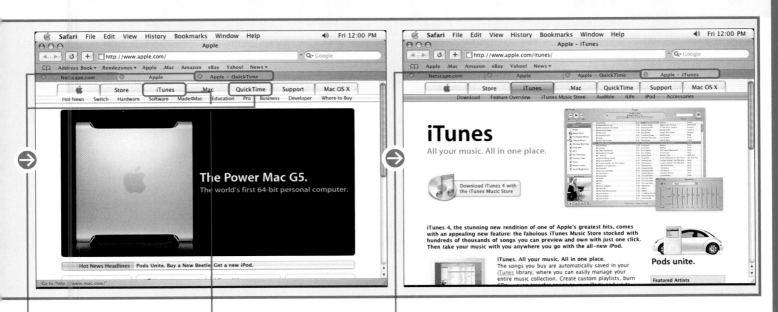

⑧ While pressing and
holding ⌘, click a Web
page link.

○ The Web site loads in a
new tab but remains in the
background.

⑨ While pressing and
holding ⌘+Shift, click a Web
page link.

○ The Web site loads in a
new tab, and the new tab
comes to the foreground.

○ You can press
⌘+Shift+Left Arrow to open
the tab to the left of the
current tab.

○ You can press
⌘+Shift+Right Arrow to
open the tab to the right of
the current tab.

○ You can press ⌘+W to
close the current tab.

DOCUMENTS IN SAFARI

Safari is a powerful and fast Web browser. Because so many people use it most often as a Web browser, it is no wonder that they often overlook the fact that Safari is also great for other daily tasks. Got an image that you want to view? Safari can display it for you. Have a movie that you would like to watch? Safari can play it, too.

What makes Safari such a great choice as a document viewer is not just that it can display content. It also has great bookmarking features.

Thus, you can organize your content just as you do Web links.

Customize It ☀

If you have countless software manuals on your hard drive, Safari makes it a snap to keep the information at your fingertips. Create a bookmark for each manual and organize them in the Bookmarks window. Without any additional software, you can have a complete documentation tool at your disposal.

① Launch Safari.

② Choose File ➪ Open and select a JPEG, GIF, PICT, or PNG image.

○ The image appears in a Safari window.

Note: Besides using the File menu, you can also drag an image file from the Finder and drop it in the Safari window to view it.

③ Click Bookmarks.

④ Click Add Bookmark.

○ Safari prompts you for a name and location for the bookmark.

Note: You can select the bookmark later by clicking the Show All Bookmarks button to view the content.

Note: Keep in mind that Safari will only be able to display the content at a later date if the content stays in the same place on your hard drive. This is a good reason to organize your files according to the Mac file structure (for example, Pictures, Movies, and so on).

SAVE WEB PAGES
on your hard drive

One of the biggest pains about saving Web pages is that they are usually composed of many different files. To save them properly, you have to save each individual part of the page. This usually means that you must know HTML and will have to look at the source code for the page. This is hardly elegant, nor particularly fun. It also has a negative side effect. Depending on how the Web page is served, this may not even work. It is an unreliable and troublesome method to save a Web page.

Panther offers a much slicker way to save Web pages. By printing to PDF, you can maintain formatting, images, and fonts and keep the whole thing saved in one file. Not only is one file easier to manage, but the PDF file looks exactly like the Web page as viewed in the browser.

① Launch Safari.

② Load a Web page.

③ Click File.

④ Click Print.

○ The Print dialog box appears.

⑤ Click Save As PDF.

○ The standard Save dialog box appears.

○ You can change the filename and location where to save the page or accept the defaults.

⑥ Click Save.

○ The Web page is saved as a PDF file.

Note: To view the page later, you can double-click it in the Finder. Preview makes a good viewer for PDF files. Keep in mind, though, that although Preview can display and act on links in PDF files, the Save As PDF button in the Print dialog box does not preserve links.

STOP POP-UP ADS
from appearing in your browser

As the Web has grown, businesses have found it harder and harder to grab your attention. To keep your eyes focused on their products, businesses have resorted to all sorts of tricks. Some of these include dirty tricks such as pop-up windows. Without you knowingly taking an action, advertisers like to display a window (usually a smaller size than most Web pages) with a small ad in it. After you surf through a couple of Web pages with this "feature," it feels like you are being bombarded with advertisements.

Safari has a great feature to help you out — the Block Pop-Up Windows option. With this option, you can block those pesky pop-up windows from ever appearing. The pop-up windows will disappear from your Web browsing landscape, leaving you with a clean appearance and a thankful wrist. Curiously, Safari has this feature set to off by default.

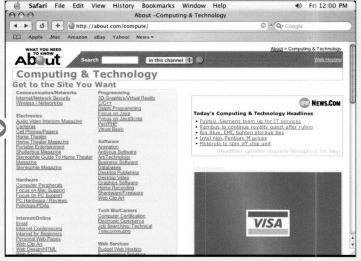

① Launch Safari.

② Load a Web page.

③ Click Safari.

④ Click Block Pop-Up Windows.

⑤ Load a Web page that usually pops up an ad window.

○ The ad does not appear.

ELIMINATE SPAM
with Mail

DIFFICULTY LEVEL

Spam is one of those things that people love to hate . . . and not without reason. Spam has taken over many people's mailboxes with ridiculous offers and scams and wastes hours of time. Fortunately, the Mail application that ships with Panther has some great utilities that help tame the beast that is spam.

Perhaps the biggest nuisance of spam is the fact that it is not always easy to determine which e-mail is spam and which is not. Through an ingenious use of color-coding, Mail makes it easy to identify spam with only a quick glance.

Customize It! ※

If you do not like the brownish shade that Mail uses to mark spam e-mail, you are free to change it. Click Mail ⇨ Preferences. In the Preferences window that appears, click the Rules button. In the Rules list, select the Junk item and click the Edit button. Change the color to one more to your liking.

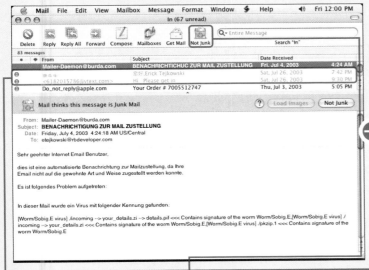

① Launch the Mail application.

② Open your Inbox.

○ Messages that Mail thinks are spam appear in a tan color in your Inbox.

③ Click the Junk icon to label e-mail as spam, should it get past the spam filters (Not Junk appears as Junk for mail not marked as spam).

④ Click Not Junk to change an e-mail marked as spam to one that is not.

Note: On occasion Mail might think that an e-mail is spam when it is not. The Not Junk button will rectify this situation.

Note: As you let Mail know which messages are spam and which are not, it learns to identify spam better as time progresses.

MANAGE
threaded
E-MAIL

When a friend sends you an e-mail and you click Reply to answer the e-mail, you are creating a *thread.* Should your friend decide to also reply, that message also becomes part of the thread. Later, when you want to review each of the messages in that thread, you have to scroll through all of your messages looking for similar subject lines. Or do you?

Panther adds a nice feature to the Mail application that helps you keep track of e-mail threads. Mail can display e-mail in a hierarchical folder arrangement, much like List view in the Finder. That way, you can backtrack through the thread and reread the previous messages that pertain to any new ones that arrive by simply expanding the thread's enclosing folder. This takes a lot of the guesswork and scrolling out of replying to e-mails.

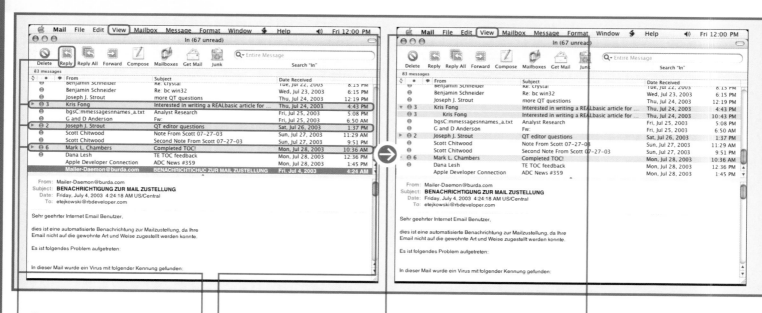

① Launch the Mail application.

② Send an e-mail to a friend or associate.

③ When the person replies, click Reply and answer the e-mail.

④ Click View.

⑤ Click Organize by Thread.

○ Threaded e-mail messages are highlighted in blue, with disclosure triangles for expanding each thread.

⑥ Click View.

⑦ Click Expand All Threads.

○ Threaded e-mail messages expand to reveal all messages in each thread.

⑧ Click View.

⑨ Click Collapse All Threads.

○ Threaded e-mail messages collapse to collapse each thread.

Set up a
WEB SERVER

DIFFICULTY LEVEL

Panther comes with a Web server installed. In fact, it is one of the most powerful Web servers around — Apache. Apache is a world-renowned Web server because it is both powerful and reliable. Besides having this power, Apache is also easy to use in Panther. One click is all it takes to start serving Web pages.

After you get your Web server running, all you have to do is add Web pages, and you are ready to roll. By default, there is a Web page installed for the machine as well as one for each user.

You can replace the default page with one of your design or edit the existing file. All machines on the local network will be able to access pages on your Web server without any additional work. For computers outside your local network, you will have to open a port on your firewall to permit the serving of Web pages.

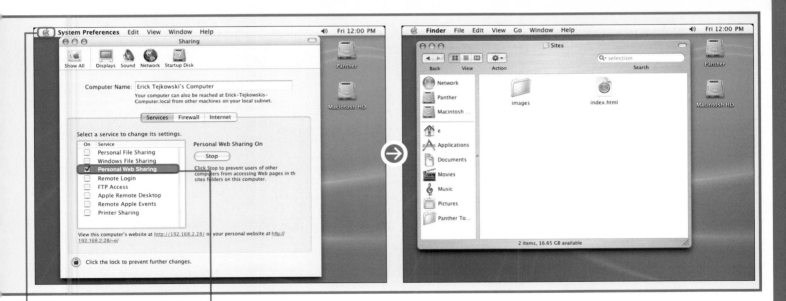

① Open System Preferences by clicking ⇨ System Preferences.

○ The System Preferences window opens.

② Click Sharing.

○ The Sharing Preferences pane opens.

③ Click Personal Web Sharing (changes to ☑).

○ The Apache Web server launches, and you are ready to serve Web pages.

④ Open a Finder window and navigate to the ~/Sites directory.

Note: This is where you should add Web pages for your personal Web page.

VISIT WEB SITES
of people in your
Address Book

The Address Book application in Panther, as you may have guessed, is a utility for storing the addresses of your family, friends, and associates. In addition to names and addresses, you can also store e-mail addresses, telephone numbers, and home pages.

The Address Book is tightly integrated with many applications in Mac OS X, including the Safari Web browser. You can view URLs that you enter into your Address Book using Safari.

Customize It ※

You can drag addresses from the Address Book section in the Bookmarks page of Safari to other bookmark folders. This is handy for organizing your various friends' and contacts' home pages with other Web pages that may pertain to them. You can also drag home page entries from the Address Book section to the Finder to create a URL file.

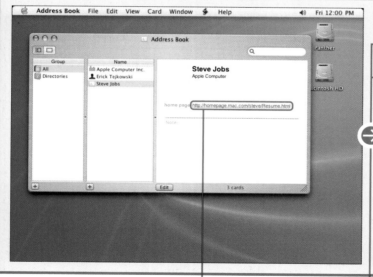

① Launch the Address Book application.

② Add an entry for a friend, making sure to complete the home page field.

③ Launch Safari.

④ Click the Bookmarks button.

○ The Bookmarks page appears.

⑤ Click the Address Book in the Collections pane.

○ The home pages of your friends appear in the View pane. Safari gets this information directly from the Address Book.

⑥ Double-click one of your friend's home pages to load it in the browser.

Use Rendezvous to SURF LOCAL WEB SITES

#84

DIFFICULTY LEVEL

If you have Mac Web sites running on your local network, you can locate them and view them with Safari. There is no need to save a bookmark for those Web sites because Safari can find them on the network for you.

Safari accomplishes this nifty trick through the magic of Rendezvous. Rendezvous is the name of the technology that Apple uses to automatically find services on a network. With Rendezvous, there is no need for IP addresses or domain names. It just finds them; it is just that simple.

Did You Know? ※

Just because you are running one Web server does not mean that only one Web site will appear in Rendezvous. The default installation of the Apache Web server in Mac OS X creates a Web site for each user on a machine as well as one for the root of the machine. So you may see as many as six Web sites if the Web server has five users.

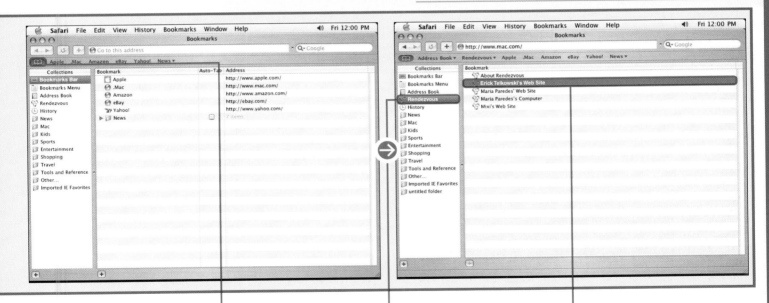

① Launch Safari.

② Open the Bookmarks page by clicking the Show All Bookmarks icon.

③ In the Collections pane, click Rendezvous.

○ Safari lists the Web sites that it finds on the network.

④ Double-click a bookmark to view that Web site.

SAVE INTERNET CONTENT
for later use

As you surf the Web, you will sometimes run into something that you want to save for later use. You may see a cool desktop image that you want to use for your own desktop or a movie trailer that you want to show a family member who is not at home.

All content that appears on a Web page is actually a file somewhere on your hard drive. The browser downloaded it to your computer so that you could view it. This means that all the content is also available for you to use later.

With Safari, you can save images, movies, and more in a number of different manners, such as downloading, copying, saving, and dragging files. None of these is a big surprise for proficient Mac users, but they may not all occur to you.

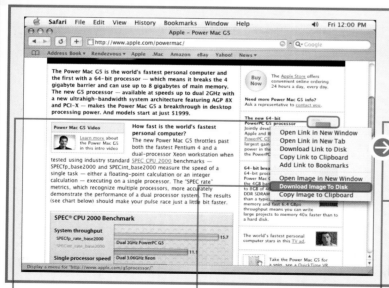

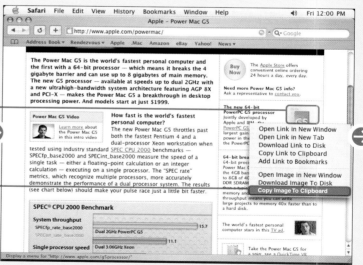

DOWNLOAD AN IMAGE

① Launch the Safari Web browser.

② Load a Web page containing an image that you want to save.

③ Control+click the image.

○ A contextual menu appears.

④ Click Download Image To Disk.

○ Safari downloads the image and saves it in your default download location — by default, the desktop, unless you have changed it.

COPY AN IMAGE

⑤ Control+click the image.

○ A contextual menu appears.

⑥ Click Copy Image to Clipboard.

Note: You can paste the image into any application that will let you do so, such as AppleWorks, Microsoft Word, or Adobe Photoshop. □

Apply It

To save QuickTime movies in Safari, click the triangle icon in the movie controller and choose Save As Source from the menu. The standard Save As dialog box appears, giving you the opportunity to save the movie on your hard drive. This does not work for all QuickTime movies, however, because some content is protected for copyright reasons by the author. In those instances, Save As Source will be dimmed.

Apply It

After you copy an image to the Clipboard in Safari, open the Preview application. Click File ⇨ New from Pasteboard to create a new image from the image on the Clipboard. After you have created a new image in Preview, you can export it to one of a dozen different formats.

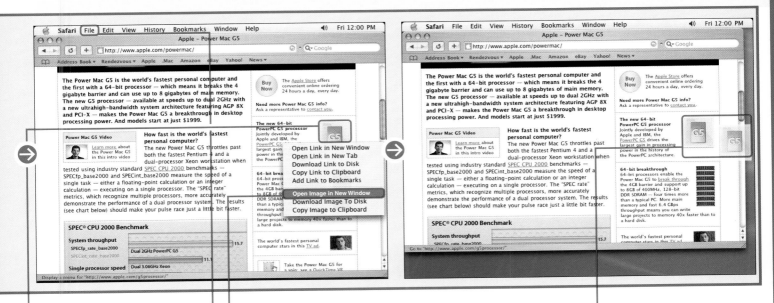

SAVE AN IMAGE WITH SAVE AS

⑦ Control+click the image.

○ A contextual menu appears.

⑧ Click Open Image in New Window.

○ A new window opens with the image in it.

⑨ Click File ⇨ Save As to save the file on your hard drive.

DRAG AN IMAGE TO THE FINDER

⑩ Load a Web page with an image that you want to save.

⑪ Drag the image directly from the Web page to the Finder.

○ The image file appears in the Finder.

Use Sherlock to
FIND INFORMATION
and perform tasks

The Internet is a great tool, but sometimes it is not so good at giving you specific information quickly. Searching for the simplest information can sometimes feel like an exercise in futility. To help you out, Apple created Sherlock. Sherlock attempts to harness some of the more common needs of the Internet for you, presents them in a convenient format, and expedites your search for information considerably.

Whereas the Internet tends to "think globally," Sherlock narrows your search and may be best

described as "acting locally." Sherlock excels at tasks such as finding schedules for your local movie theater, looking up phone numbers for the pizza place down the street, or looking up the meaning of a word.

Sherlock comes with a number of useful utilities, but it can do so much more. Sherlock uses a plug-in format that permits third-party users to extend the functionality of Sherlock. This has led to a proliferation of Sherlock plug-ins that help you do everything from troubleshooting your Macintosh to shopping online.

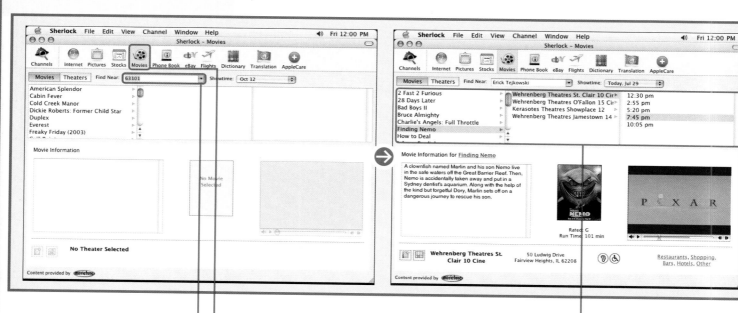

FIND MOVIES

① Open the Applications folder and double-click the Sherlock icon.

○ The main Sherlock interface opens.

② Click Movies.

○ The Movies interface opens.

③ Type the name of a city or its zip code to find movies playing near your home.

④ Press Return to see the results.

○ Sherlock scours the Internet for you and finds the names of all movies playing in your area. It also displays the times and locations where you can see them.

Apply It

Many useful Sherlock plug-ins are available on the Internet. You will find plug-ins for searching commercial sites, government sites, and Mac sites. You can track packages, find sheet music for your favorite tunes, and read tutorials. Sherlock can do it all. For examples, check out the Web site Sherlock Plug-ins for Power Users (http://pwrsearchr.users1.50megs.com/sherlock/pg1.html). This Web site makes a good jumping-off point for seeing what Sherlock plug-ins are available.

Customize It!

If you would like to move a Sherlock plug-in icon in the toolbar, press and hold ⌘ while you drag the icon to its new location in the toolbar.

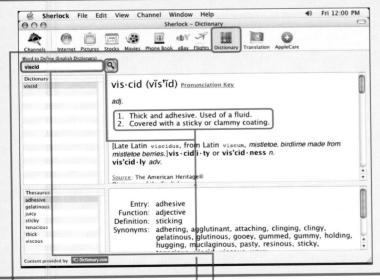

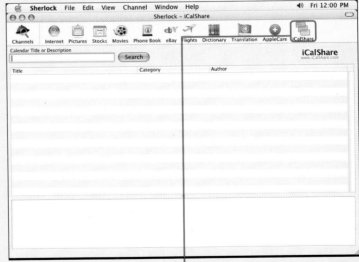

LOOK UP WORDS IN THE DICTIONARY

① Click the Dictionary button.

○ The Dictionary interface opens.

② Type a word that you would like to look up.

③ Click the search button.

○ Sherlock looks the word up for you and gives you the full definition.

USE A PLUG-IN

① To install a plug-in, simply click the link on the Web site where the plug-in is located.

○ The plug-in self-installs in Sherlock.

Note: The iCalShare (www.icalshare.com) We Speak Sherlock calendar plug-in is shown here.

○ After Sherlock installs a new plug-in, you can instantly use it by clicking its icon in the Sherlock toolbar.

Channel the power of the
ADDRESS BOOK
IN MAIL

The Address Book application in Panther is a central repository for all your contact information. It stores names, addresses, telephone numbers, e-mail addresses, and many other bits of information. The Address Book does a good job of helping you organize all of this information, but this is only part of its true power. The Address Book can also play nicely with the rest of the applications on your Mac. Rather than have this type of data stored multiple times in different applications, it makes sense to store it once in the Address Book. From there, the other applications can access the information. Many different applications already support the Address Book protocol.

For example, the Address Book works in conjunction with the Mail application. If you enter e-mail addresses for your various contacts in the Address Book, you can use them in Mail to send e-mails.

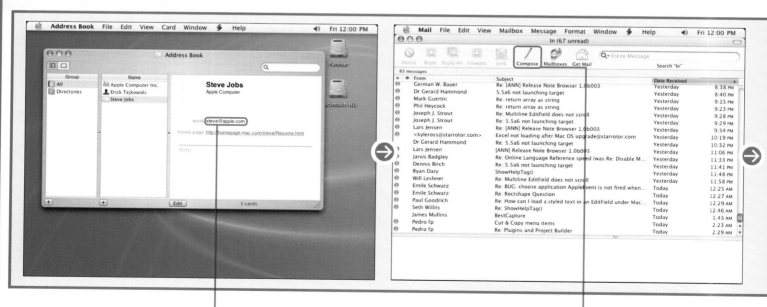

① Launch the Address Book application.

② Add an entry for a friend, making sure to complete the e-mail field.

③ Launch Mail.

④ Click Compose.

DIFFICULTY LEVEL

Customize It ※

To export an address from the Addresses window in Mail, ⌘+click the person's name whom you would like to export. Choose the Export Vcard menu item to save the address as a file. You can attach this Vcard file to send e-mail addresses from your Address Book to others.

Did You Know? ※

As you use the addresses in Mail, you can continue to make changes to the Address Book application. When you switch back to Mail, its address list reflects the changes that you made in the Address Book.

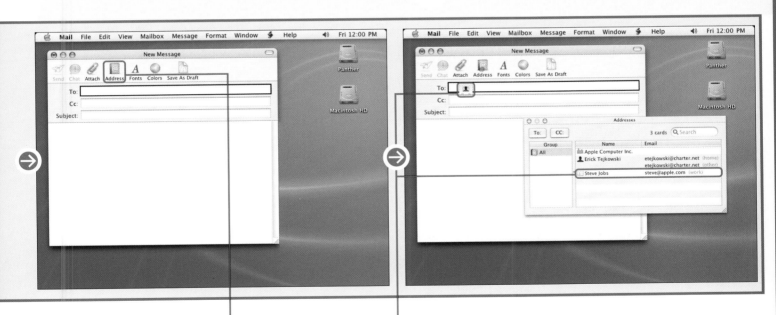

○ A new blank e-mail message appears.

⑤ Click the Address Book.

○ The e-mail addresses of your friends appear in the Addresses window.

⑥ Drag a name from the Addresses window to the To: or Cc: fields of the e-mail message.

○ The e-mail address instantly appears in the field.

Note: You can continue dragging and dropping other names to the To: and Cc: fields if you need to e-mail more than one person at a time.

CHAPTER 8

Making the Most of Your Network Connection

Ever since the Internet boom of the 1990s, it seems that everyone and everything is networked. Mac OS X Panther keeps pace with all the latest networking developments. With Panther, you can use the network to share files with Macintosh and Microsoft Windows computers as well as devices such as the iPod.

File sharing is just one of the many uses of a network connection available to you in Panther. Using iChat, you can trade files, exchange text messages, and even teleconference with full-motion video and high-quality audio. With iTunes, you can turn your network into a jukebox instantly. Using practically any application, you can send faxes to anywhere in the world.

Besides communication and multimedia, the network is great for utility purposes. Using the Terminal application, you can remotely control other computers on the network, repair a frozen Mac, and even peek at hidden files on an iPod. Panther supports all sorts of networking protocols and even has a built-in software firewall.

Printing is yet another perfect use for your network. With a few simple clicks, you can share printers on the network. This gives multiple computers on the network the option of printing with the same printer.

TOP 100

#88 Share music over your network
with iTunes................................134

#89 Audio and video conferencing
with iChat.................................135

#90 Share music on a network drive.........136

#91 Download files with FTP................138

#92 Remotely control other computers on
your network..............................140

#93 Protect your computer with a firewall.....142

#94 Share files with Windows computers.......143

#95 Share printers with other computers.......144

#96 Unfreeze a frozen Mac over the network....146

#97 Share files with iChat..................148

#98 Use iChat keyboard shortcuts...........150

#99 Fax files from any application...........151

#100 Share an iPod on a network...........152

Connecting to Network

SHARE MUSIC
over your network
WITH ITUNES

DIFFICULTY LEVEL

With iTunes and a network, you can turn your Mac into a jukebox without doing much work at all. iTunes is already a sort of jukebox for your personal music, but iTunes also has a great sharing feature that lets you listen to music on any Mac on the network.

After you activate iTunes sharing, you can listen to music that is located on other Macs on your network. Likewise, other Macs can listen to your music. The Source list of the iTunes interface lists the shared tunes and even displays the other users' playlists.

Customize It ☀

Because iTunes shares your playlists, you might consider other possible uses for them. For example, you can make a playlist customized for each member of your family or your coworkers at the office. Further, by activating and deactivating playlists in the Sharing pane of the iTunes Preferences window, you can restrict which elements of your library that you want to share.

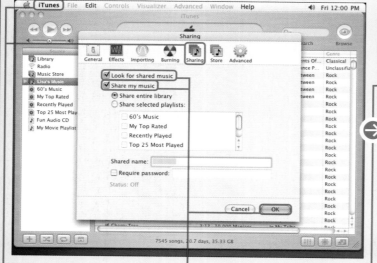

ACTIVATE SHARING

1. Launch iTunes.
2. Click iTunes.
3. Click Preferences.
4. Click Sharing.

○ The Sharing pane of the Preferences window appears.

5. Click Look for Shared Music (☐ changes to ☑).
6. Click Share My Music (☐ changes to ☑).
7. Click OK.

PLAY MUSIC ON YOUR NETWORK

8. Locate shared music on your local network in the Source list.

Note: Shared music servers appear with a blue icon.

9. Click the song that you would like to hear.
10. Click the Play button.

○ The song begins to play.

AUDIO AND VIDEO
conferencing
WITH ICHAT

DIFFICULTY LEVEL

You can use iChat to talk to your friends, family, and coworkers. Connect a microphone and a camera to have your iChat buddies see and hear you. Many cameras, such as Apple's iSight, have built-in microphones, so you have to connect only a camera. If you do not have a camera but you do have a microphone, you can chat with audio only. If your buddies have neither a camera nor a microphone, they can still see and hear you, even if you cannot see and hear them.

Did You Know? ※

The iChat application is compatible with AOL Instant Messenger and uses its network for communication, but it can also function on its own without the AOL network. Using Rendezvous, you can connect and talk to people on your local network without ever logging in to AOL's network.

① In a Finder window, click your Applications folder.

② Double-click iChat.

○ iChat launches.

③ Locate friends who have audio and video capabilities in the Buddy list.

Note: AV-capable machines on the network have small camera and audio icons next to the buddy name.

④ Double-click the AV icon of the buddy with whom you want to chat.

○ iChat invites your buddy to a multimedia chat.

Connecting
to Network

SHARE MUSIC
on a network drive

To share music with another Mac on your network, you can mount a shared drive on that Mac using the Finder. After you have the drive mounted, it acts like any other drive on your machine. Add music to your iTunes Library as you normally would, but use the networked drive instead.

The benefit of this method versus the automatic sharing in iTunes is flexibility. By sharing music on a shared drive, you can add items on the remote computer to your own playlists. You can also edit information about a song, such as its title and artist.

To begin playing music, choose the song that you want to hear and click the Play button. On an ethernet network, iTunes streams the audio perfectly. In fact, iTunes is so good at streaming that you can even use an old Mac as a music server. Even though the old Mac may not support the latest version of OS X, if it can support an HFS+ drive (Mac OS 8 and later), you can use it with your slick Panther machine.

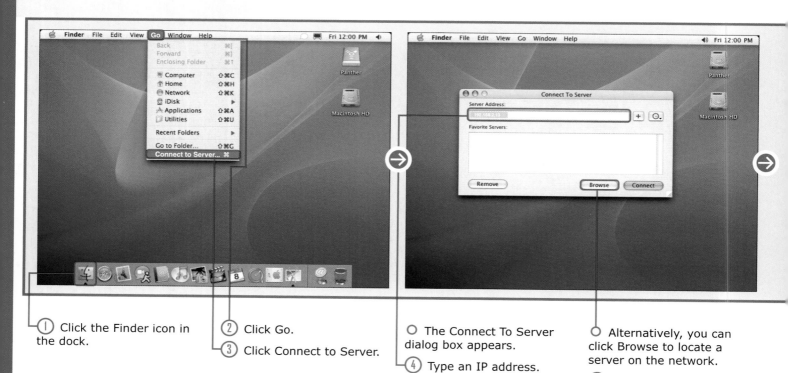

① Click the Finder icon in the dock.

② Click Go.

③ Click Connect to Server.

○ The Connect To Server dialog box appears.

④ Type an IP address.

○ Alternatively, you can click Browse to locate a server on the network.

⑤ Choose a shared drive from one of the available servers.

#90

DIFFICULTY LEVEL

Caution! ⁂

Do not rely on the speed of
network traffic when burning a CD
in iTunes. Although it is technically
possible to burn a CD using files over
the network, you cannot always guarantee
that a network is going to behave as fast as
possible. Therefore, it is a good idea to copy files
from remote computers to your Mac before trying to
burn them to a CD. By using local files, you can avoid
problems with burned disks. This can also accelerate the
burning process.

Did You Know? ⁂

Sharing music with another computer is fun, but
sharing music with two computers is twice as fun.
As your music collection grows and your available
hard drive space decreases, you can store files on
other computers on the network.

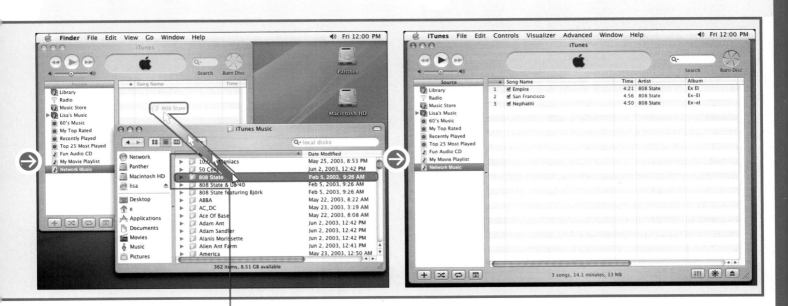

⑥ After you have mounted
a shared drive, locate the
music files on that drive.

⑦ Drag the music files from
the remote drive to iTunes to
add them to the library.

⑧ After you add files to
iTunes from a remote server,
you can create playlists
based on those files.

DOWNLOAD
files with FTP

The next time that you click to download from an FTP link in Safari, do not be alarmed if you cannot find the downloaded file. Behind the scenes, the Finder is mounting a drive on your Mac. You can then retrieve the file from that mounted drive.

The Finder works well for downloading files from your own FTP servers. The downside is that it is a one-way-only process. You cannot upload files to an FTP server in the Finder. To upload to an FTP server,

you could use the "old school" method and use the command line. Alternatively, you could opt for a slick GUI-based FTP client. There are many available on the Internet, including some good free ones.

Do not forget that Panther comes with an FTP server built-in. Launch it by using the Sharing pane of System Preferences. After the FTP server is launched, users can log in and share files with you.

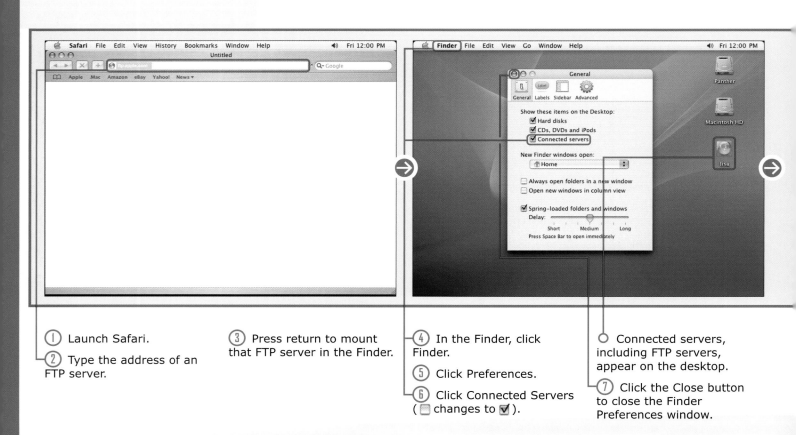

① Launch Safari.

② Type the address of an FTP server.

③ Press return to mount that FTP server in the Finder.

④ In the Finder, click Finder.

⑤ Click Preferences.

⑥ Click Connected Servers (☐ changes to ☑).

○ Connected servers, including FTP servers, appear on the desktop.

⑦ Click the Close button to close the Finder Preferences window.

Customize It

When you activate your FTP server, users will have access to the files located in the ~/Library/Public folder. You are free to add and remove folders and files to this folder to customize your FTP downloads.

DIFFICULTY LEVEL

Did You Know?

FTP is over 30 years old! Included as one of the technologies in ARPANet, a military precursor to the Internet, FTP has been serving millions of files for years. Do not let its old age fool you, though. Age means that it is well tested, debugged, and competent. UNIX, upon which Mac OS X Panther sits, is also aged. The software has continued to improve over the years, naturally, but the roots are planted far in the past. Its age has led to its reputation for reliable multiuser performance.

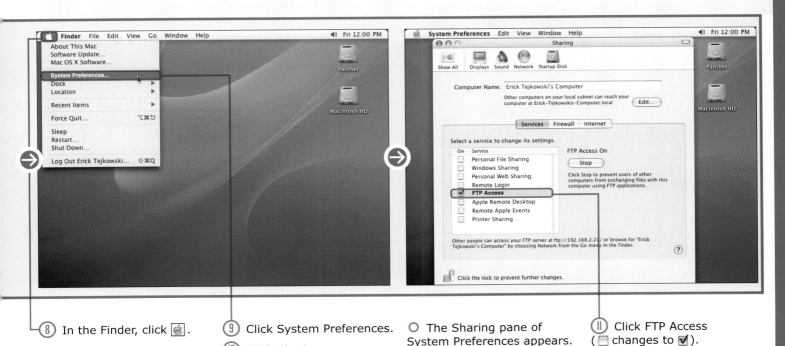

⑧ In the Finder, click .

⑨ Click System Preferences.

⑩ Click Sharing.

○ The Sharing pane of System Preferences appears.

⑪ Click FTP Access (☐ changes to ☑).

○ The FTP server is activated.

Remotely CONTROL OTHER COMPUTERS
on your network

You can remotely control other computers on the network in much the same way as your own. Using the command-line application Terminal and the command-line program ssh, you can remotely launch applications, work with files, and even shut down computers without walking into another room.

Before you get started remotely controlling a remote computer, you need to take one last walk to it and activate remote access for it. You will also need to make sure that you have an account on the remote machine.

Back on your own computer, launch the Terminal application. Now you are ready to control the remote machine with ssh. ssh ships with Mac OS X Panther; it is a command-line-only program and has no graphical user interface. You can read all about ssh by typing **man ssh**.

When you connect to a remote computer, it is as if you are sitting in front of it — almost. You cannot use the mouse to control the remote machine with ssh, but you can use any installed command-line program. For example, you can launch iTunes by typing only two lines of text in Terminal.

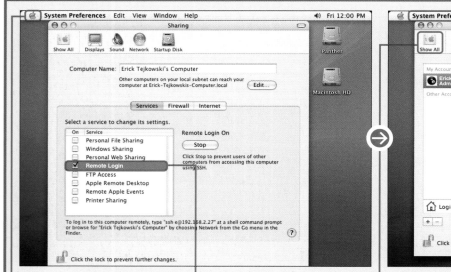

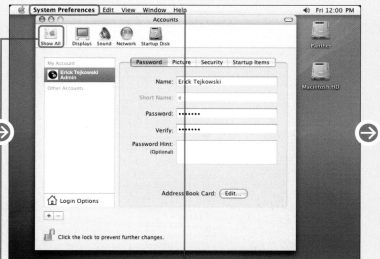

① On the remote computer, click .

② Click System Preferences.

○ The System Preferences window opens.

③ Click Sharing.

○ The Sharing pane of System Preferences appears.

④ Click Remote Login (changes to ☑).

○ The computer is now enabled for remote access.

⑤ Write down the IP address of the remote computer, which appears in the Sharing pane.

⑥ Click Show All.

⑦ Click Accounts.

○ The Accounts pane appears.

Note: Make certain that you have an account on this computer by adding another user. If you are remotely controlling a computer in a business, ask a system administrator for permission first.

⑧ Click System Preferences ⇨ Quit.

DIFFICULTY LEVEL

Caution! ※

The ssh tool is extremely powerful; in the wrong hands, it can cause considerable problems for you. Create accounts in System Preferences only for trustworthy people. You should also restrict administrative accounts to those whom you especially trust. It is a common security principle that a safe machine is a disconnected machine. Whenever you are not using remote login, it is a good idea to deactivate it in the Sharing pane of System Preferences. The "bad guys" cannot connect via ssh if you have this turned off. The same holds true for all items in the Sharing pane. If you are not using the FTP server, turn it off. Your machine will be more secure, and it will eat up less CPU power.

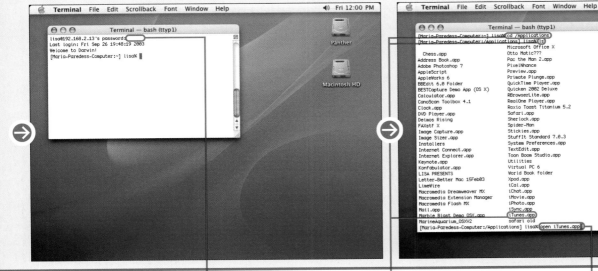

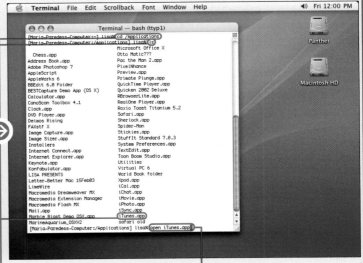

⑨ In the Finder of the local computer, click Go ⇨ Applications.

⑩ Open the Utilities folder and double-click Terminal.

○ The Terminal application launches.

⑪ Type **ssh –l username 127.0.0.1**, where username is your account on the remote computer and 127.0.0.1 is the IP address of the remote computer.

⑫ Press Return.

⑬ When prompted, enter your password and press Return.

⑭ Type **cd /Applications**.

⑮ Type **ls**.

⑯ Make sure that iTunes.app appears in the list of applications.

⑰ Type **open iTunes.app** to launch iTunes on the remote machine.

PROTECT YOUR COMPUTER
with a firewall

#93

DIFFICULTY LEVEL

You can protect your computer from hackers by using a firewall. A firewall can be either a piece of hardware or a software-based solution. Mac OS X Panther has a built-in firewall that you can use to protect your computer from others. As its name implies, a *firewall* erects a "wall" on your network between you and the outside world. You can get past this wall going out, but those on the outside cannot enter.

Caution! ※

Follow good security practices when using a firewall. If you are not using a *port,* a kind of "doorway" that either blocks traffic or allows it through, there is no need to open it. Deactivate any ports that you are not using. Going back to the wall analogy — closing a port on the firewall is not like locking that doorway; instead, it is like completely removing the door from the wall.

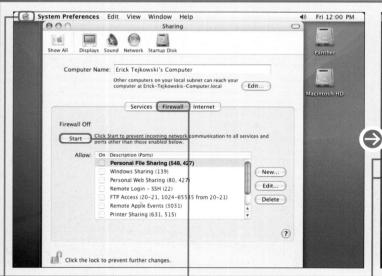

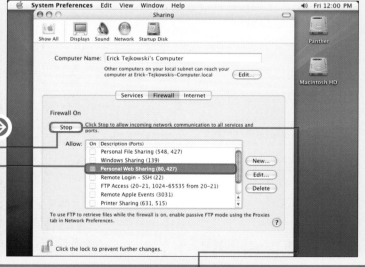

① Click .

② Click System Preferences.

③ Click Sharing.

○ The Sharing pane of System Preferences appears.

④ Click Firewall.

⑤ Click Start.

○ The firewall is activated.

⑥ Click Stop to deactivate the firewall.

⑦ Click Personal Web Sharing (changes to ✔) to permit outsiders to use its port.

⑧ Click Start.

○ The firewall is activated with the Personal Web sharing port open. Users outside of your local network can now view pages on your Web server.

SHARE FILES WITH WINDOWS
computers

#94

DIFFICULTY LEVEL

Mac OS X Panther can readily share files with both Macintosh and Microsoft Windows computers. Panther uses the technology named Samba behind the scenes to communicate with Windows computers, which makes them appear much like a Mac on the network.

You can activate Windows file sharing in the Sharing pane of System Preferences. Once activated, you can view Windows files in the Finder: Shared Windows files will appear in a Finder window if you click the Browse button.

Otherwise, you are free to connect directly to the Windows machine by means of its IP address.

You can turn on file sharing for a particular folder in Windows by right-clicking its icon. From the pop-up menu that appears, choose Sharing and Security. In the window that appears, you can activate sharing for the folder as well as assign a name for that folder on the network. This is the name that you see when viewing the network in the Finder.

① Click Go.

② Click Connect to Server.

○ A network dialog box appears, permitting you to connect to your servers.

③ If you are not sure which server you want, click Browse.

○ A Finder window appears, showing you the available computers on the network to which you can connect.

④ Double-click a server to connect to it.

─○ Mounted drives from another server may appear on the desktop.

⑤ Double-click to use them as you would any other drive.

⑥ If no drives appear on the desktop, open a Finder window to navigate to the mounted drives.

SHARE PRINTERS
with other computers

You can share printers on your network. This enables you to use one printer with multiple computers. Because printers are devices that you probably do not use continuously, it makes sense to share them with other users on the network. Sharing printers can save you time and money. You do not have to invest extra money in multiple printers, and you get more work done because you are not always running into another room to print on another computer.

You can activate printer sharing in the Sharing pane of System Preferences. If you activate Windows sharing, even Microsoft Windows computers can print to shared Mac printers.

When printer sharing is activated, other users on the network can access shared printers by using the standard Print dialog box. Panther supports a wide array of printers, but only if you install their drivers. The Panther installation disks contain numerous print drivers for you to use.

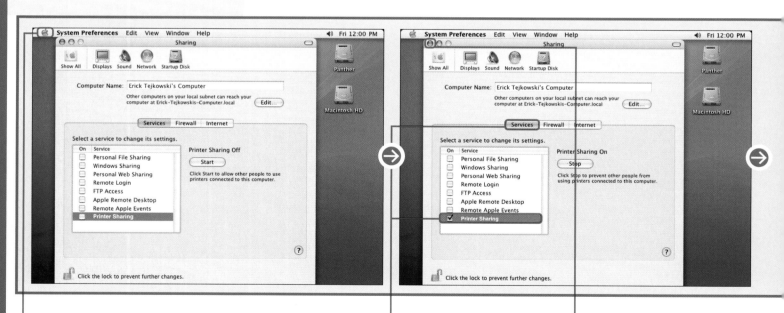

① Click .

② Click System Preferences.

○ The System Preferences window opens.

③ Click Sharing.

○ The Sharing pane of System Preferences appears.

④ Click Services.

⑤ Click Printer Sharing (changes to ✓).

○ Printer sharing is activated.

⑥ Click the Close button to close System Preferences.

Did You Know? ※

As soon as you click the Print button to commence printing, the Print Center application takes over the print job. It takes care of printing the document in the background so that you can continue working in other applications.

Caution! ※

If you make a mistake and print the wrong document, click the Print Center icon in the dock to bring it to the foreground. In the Print Center, you can cancel jobs or even deactivate printing altogether. If the printer has some sort of technical problem, you will also find alerts about the problem in the Print Center. The alerts help you diagnose and repair the problem.

DIFFICULTY LEVEL

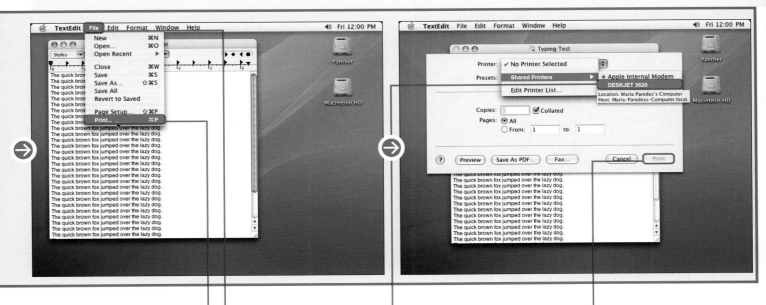

⑦ Open a document on another computer on the network to print.

⑧ Click File.

⑨ Click Print.

○ The Print dialog box appears.

⑩ Select a shared printer on the network from the Printer pop-up menu.

⑪ Click Print.

○ The document prints on the networked printer.

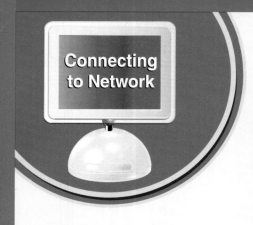
Unfreeze a
FROZEN MAC
over the network

Even with the power of UNIX behind them, computers can still sometimes act up. When an application crashes or hangs, you can force it to quit by pressing ⌘+Option+Escape or by Option+clicking its icon in the dock. However, sometimes even these strategies will not "thaw" a frozen Mac. Using the Terminal application via another computer on the network, though, you can log in to the offending machine and manually stop whatever is freezing your Mac.

The easiest way to remotely connect to another Mac on a network is to use a tool called ssh. It permits you to connect to another machine and issue it commands as if you were actually sitting in front of the machine. The ssh tool operates in a secure fashion, so you can be reasonably certain that other users on the network will not be able to "watch" your activities as you work.

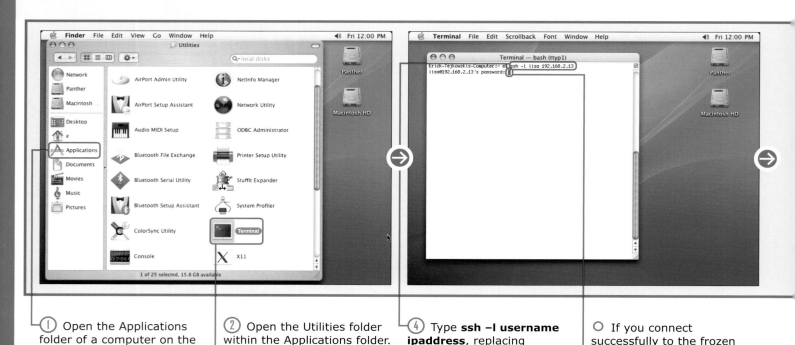

① Open the Applications folder of a computer on the network that is not locked up.

② Open the Utilities folder within the Applications folder.

③ Double-click Terminal.

④ Type **ssh -l username ipaddress**, replacing username with your account name on the frozen computer and ipaddress with the IP address of the computer.

○ If you connect successfully to the frozen networked computer, it will ask you for a valid password.

⑤ Type your password and press Return.

Put It Together ☀

Before you can unfreeze a computer over the network, you must first activate Remote Login in the Sharing pane of System Preferences; see task #92 for more information. Use safe networking practices when activating the powerful Remote Login features in Panther.

DIFFICULTY LEVEL

Caution! ☀

You should be very careful when you use the kill command. Killing the wrong process can have an adverse effect on the operation of your Mac. If you manage to screw things up beyond hope, you can always restart the frozen Mac.

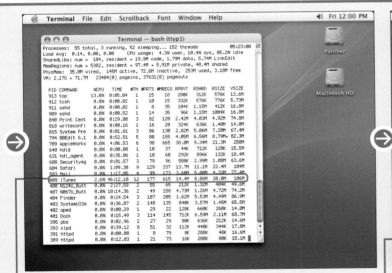

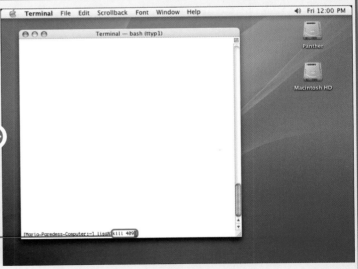

⑥ Type **top** to see what processes are currently running on the remote machine.

⑦ Look for the process that is causing the machine to become unresponsive and note its PID number.

Note: You can often tell which process is the culprit by looking at the CPU column. If one of the numbers seems especially large, that may be the offending process.

⑧ Press Control+C to stop the top program.

⑨ Type **kill pidnumber**, replacing pidnumber with the PID.

○ The process that you chose is forced to quit. If you correctly chose the offending process, the unresponsive machine becomes responsive again.

SHARE FILES
with iChat

You can send and receive files with iChat. When chatting with a buddy, you can send a file to that person in one of two ways.

The simplest way to send a file to someone is to drag it from the Finder and drop it in the text box of the chat window. When you drop the file in the box where you type text, an icon appears in the chat text box representing that file.

You can also send a file to someone in your Buddy or Rendezvous list by using the Buddies menu or a contextual menu.

Sharing files in iChat is great for exchanging photographs, short movie clips, résumés, or even homework with friends, coworkers, or schoolmates. You could send the same files with e-mail, but transferring files with iChat is much more immediate. You do not have to wait for your e-mail to bounce around all over the world until it reaches its destination. iChat sends the file directly to your recipient, who can in turn use it immediately.

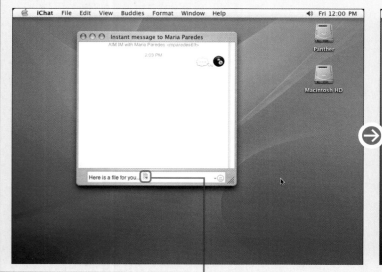

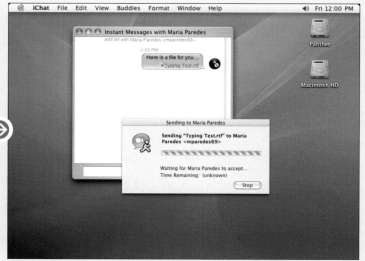

SEND A FILE USING DRAG AND DROP

① Launch iChat and initiate a chat session with a buddy to whom you would like to send a file.

② Drag a file from the Finder into the text box at the bottom of your Chat window.

③ Press Return.

○ iChat begins transferring the file to your buddy.

DIFFICULTY LEVEL

Did You Know? ☀

One of the great things about transferring files with iChat is that you are not hampered by the file size limits that you usually encounter when sending files by e-mail. There does not seem to be a limit — at least not within reason — to what size iChat can transfer. E-mail, on the other hand, often tops out at a few megabytes.

Caution! ☀

Sometimes iChat can be finicky about sending certain types of files. If you run into a circumstance in which iChat will not cooperate, try compressing the file in question first. You can use almost any compression format, such as StuffIt, ZIP, and TAR, as long as the recipient has a decompression application. Try resending the newly compressed file instead of the original.

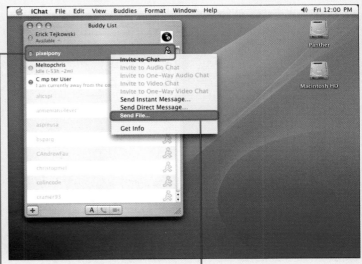

SEND A FILE USING THE BUDDIES MENU

① Click a buddy in the Buddy list to whom you would like to send a file.

② Click Buddies.

③ Click Send File.

○ iChat opens a standard file dialog box.

④ Choose the file to send.

⑤ Click OK.

○ iChat begins transferring the file to your buddy.

SEND A FILE USING A CONTEXTUAL MENU

① Control+click the name of a buddy to whom you would like to send a file.

○ A contextual menu appears.

② Click Send File.

○ iChat opens a standard file dialog box.

③ Choose the file to send.

④ Click OK.

○ iChat begins transferring the file to your buddy.

Use ICHAT keyboard SHORTCUTS

#98

DIFFICULTY LEVEL

You can speed up your iChat use with a variety of handy keyboard shortcuts. Some shortcuts help you organize your chat sessions, whereas others make features easier to use.

One keyboard shortcut permits you to type a multiline message without waiting for the text to wrap. This forces the message text box to grow by one line.

For quick entry of the numerous smiley faces, you can type the standard keyboard shortcuts. By not resorting to the mouse, you can save yourself time and effort.

Customize It

You can customize the background of your chat windows by selecting View ➪ Set Chat Background. You can also access this feature by Control+clicking in the View section of the chat window itself. If you get tired of the customized background, you can deactivate it by choosing View ➪ Clear Background.

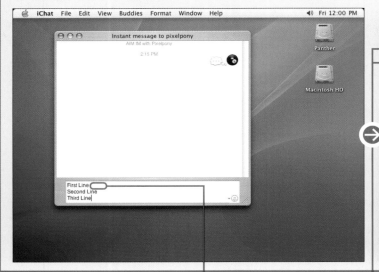

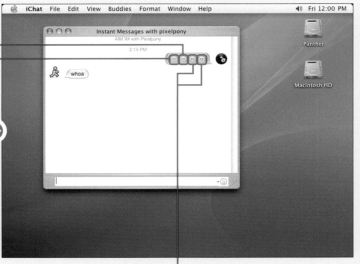

① Launch iChat and start a chat with a buddy.

② As you type a message in the chat window, press Option+Return.

○ A line break is inserted in the message, but what you have typed is not sent yet.

③ Type more text and press Return.

○ iChat sends the multiline message.

④ Type :-).

○ A smiley face appears.

⑤ Type ;-).

○ A winking smiley face appears.

⑥ Type :-D.

○ A grinning smiley face appears.

⑦ Type :-(.

○ A frowning face appears.

FAX FILES
from any application

 # 99

DIFFICULTY LEVEL

If you fax lots of files from your Mac, you will be glad to know that faxing got a lot easier in Panther. In the past, you had to rely on third-party software to send faxes, but Panther has built-in fax capabilities. This gives you the ability to fax documents from any application.

To fax a document, you use the new Fax pane of the standard Print dialog box.

Customize It ※

You can add a recipient to your fax based on entries in your Address Book. To do so, click the button with a shadow of a person next to the To field in the Fax pane of the Print dialog box. A list of entries from your Address Book appears, from which you can choose the fax recipient.

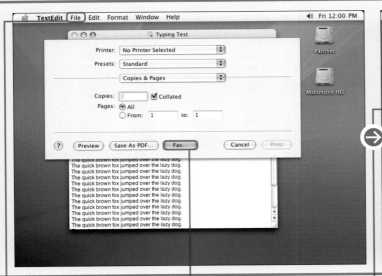

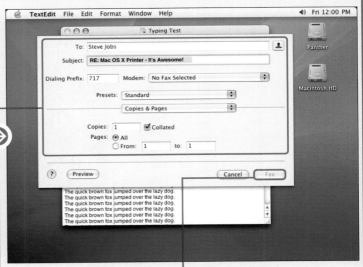

① Open a document in your favorite word processor or graphics application — even a Web page will work here.

② Click File.

③ Click Print.

○ Alternatively, you can press ⌘+P.

○ The standard Print dialog box appears.

④ Click Fax.

○ The Fax dialog box appears.

⑤ Adjust the fax settings to your preferences.

Note: You can even create a cover page for the fax.

⑥ Click Fax.

○ The fax is transmitted.

Connecting to Network

SHARE AN IPOD
on a network

You can share music on an iPod with other Macs on your network. An iPod, after all, is really just a souped-up disk drive. To begin sharing an iPod with others on the network, activate Personal File Sharing in the Sharing pane of System Preferences. Then plug an iPod into your Mac. Now other users on the network can access your drive.

When you share an iPod, other users will see the contents of the drive. They will not, however, see the music that you have uploaded to the iPod with iTunes. This does not mean that the music files are not there; they are simply hidden from view. You just have to know where to look. You can use the Terminal application to view the contents of the hidden music folder — Terminal is good at "seeing" hidden files. You can also use Terminal to perform operations on those files just as you would any other files.

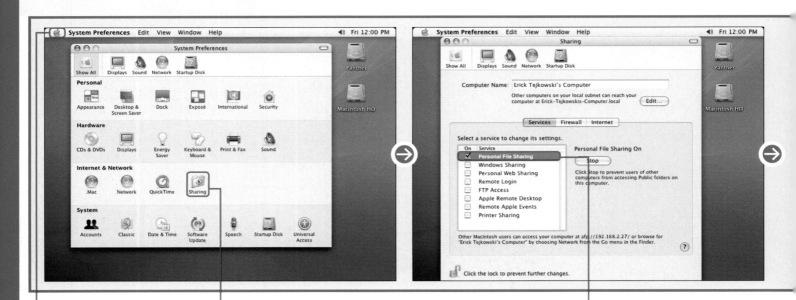

① Connect an iPod to a remote Macintosh on your local network.

② Click [icon].

③ Click System Preferences.

○ The System Preferences dialog box opens.

④ Click Sharing.

○ The Sharing pane of System Preferences appears.

⑤ Click Personal File Sharing (□ changes to ☑).

○ File sharing is activated.

Did You Know? ※

An iPod has a text file on it that stores important information about the system and its drive. You can find the file in iPodDrive/iPod_Control/ Device/SysInfo, where iPodDrive is the name of an iPod when mounted on the desktop. Open the SysInfo file with a text editor such as TextEdit to view its contents. You may recognize the text within the file because the iPod is capable of displaying the same information.

Apply It ※

To view the SysInfo text on the iPod, press the Menu button repeatedly until you locate the main menu. From there, scroll the wheel until you find About in the list of choices. Click the center button on the iPod to view the About window for the iPod. The About window displays the text found in the SysInfo file.

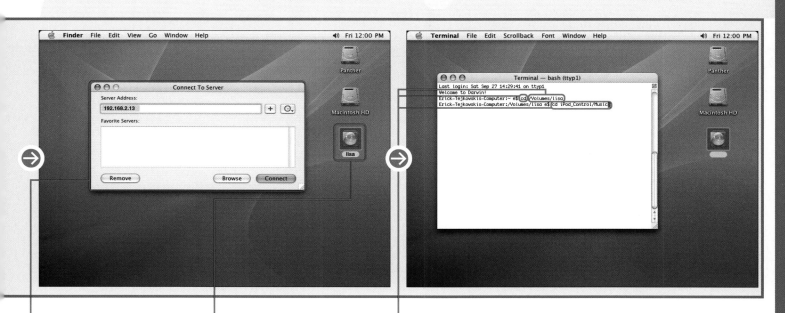

⑥ Go to a different Macintosh on the same local network and press ⌘+K.

⑦ Mount the shared iPod volume just as you would any other shared drive.

Note: See task #90 for more information.

○ The remote iPod drive mounts on the machine.

⑧ Launch Terminal.

⑨ Type **cd** and then drag the iPod drive from the Finder into Terminal.

○ The path to the iPod appears.

⑩ Press Return.

⑪ Type **cd iPod_Control/Music** and press Return.

○ Terminal changes directory to the location of the iPod's hidden music files.

⑫ Type **ls** and press Return.

○ A list of directories appears. Within each of these are the hidden music files.

153

INDEX

Symbols and Numbers

 menu
About This Mac command, 104
Force Quit command, 100
Recent Items list, 47
Restart command, 108
Sleep command, 48
24-hour clock display, 11

A

AAC format, convert files to, 80
About This Mac command (menu), 104
Accounts pane (System Preferences), 49, 65
Acrobat (Adobe), 56
Acrobat Reader (Adobe), 67
Activity Monitor, 105
Address Book application
add entry, 124, 130
customize My Card, 69
fax recipients in, 151
with Mail, 130–131
overview, 124, 130
surf Web sites for people in, 124
Admin account, 111
Adobe
Acrobat, 56
Acrobat Reader, 67
Photoshop, 87
AIFF Encoder dialog box, 80
AIFF format, convert files to, 80, 97
Aladdin Systems Spring Cleaning, 109
albums (iPhoto), 94, 95
alerts
Flash Screen effect, 17
select sound, 12–13
aliases, 34–35
Alsoft DiskWarrior, 108
Always Open With option, 31
Analog clock configuration, 10–11
announcement feature for time, 10
AOL Instant Messenger, 135
Apache Web server, 123, 125
Appearance color, 7
Appearance pane (System Preferences), 7, 9
Apple Help Viewer list, 101
Apple menu ()
About This Mac command, 104
Force Quit command, 100
Recent Items list, 47
Restart command, 108
Sleep command, 48
AppleCare Knowledge Base, 106
AppleScript for CDs and DVDs, 54
AppleWorks versus TextEdit, 74
applications. See also specific applications
add keyboard shortcut, 53
bookmark manuals in Safari, 118
choose for files, 31

commercial uninstall utility, 109
fax files from, 151
force to quit, 100, 146–147
Help topics from, 101
launch for CDs and DVDs, 54
launch recent items, 47
Services menu commands, 55
Startup items, 50, 65
switch with dock, 26
switch with Exposé, 46
System Profiler information for, 104
uninstall, 109
Applications folder on Go menu, 52
appointments, share with portable devices, 72
ARPANet (Internet precursor), 139
audio aids, 16–17
audio CDs
burn with iTunes, 82–83
capacity, 83
choose action for, 54
convert files, 80
import tracks to iTunes, 78–79
audio conferencing with iChat, 135
audio files. See music; sounds
automatic features
check for updates, 107
desktop image change, 6
hide dock, 45
login, 111
startup, 50, 65
AVI format for QuickTime movies, 92

B

background of desktop
add your own, 4–5
change automatically, 6
Fill Screen versus Tile option, 5
focus aided by change to, 2
Block Pop-Up Windows feature, 120
Bluetooth devices, iSync with, 60
bookmarks (Safari), 118, 124
booting. See also launching or running
from CD-ROM, 103, 108
display system boot menu, 108
multiple Mac OS versions, 68
browser. See Safari Web browser
Buddies menu (iChat), 149
burning discs
audio CDs with iTunes, 82–83
data CDs with iTunes, 82
DVDs with iDVD, 81
DVDs with iTunes, 82–83
using files over network, 137
Burns, Ken (filmmaker), 90
button colors, change, 7

C

Capture command (Grab menu), 71
Card menu (Address Book), 69

cd **command (UNIX), 62, 153**
CD drives
    boot from, 103, 108
    burn CDs with iTunes, 82–83
    capacity of discs, 83
    choose action for CDs, 54
    in Finder Places sidebar, 18, 22
    format discs, 54
    hide icons on desktop, 15
cellphones, 60, 72
Choose Application dialog box, 31
Classic mode, 112–113
Classic pane (System Preferences), 112–113
Clear Background command (iChat View menu), 150
Clipboard, copy image from Internet to, 126
closing. *See also* **quitting**
    force program to quit, 100, 146–147
    Safari tabs, 117
Color Label command, 29
colors
    custom, 7
    labels, 29
    remove (grayscale display), 17
    spam in Mail application, 121
Colors palette, 7
Column view, 18, 37
command line. *See* **Terminal application (UNIX); UNIX**
compression formats, 149
contextual menus
    access commands, 25
    Color Label command, 29
    Copy *"Filename"* command, 33
    Copy Image to Clipboard command, 126
    Duplicate command, 32
    Finder, 25
    Make Alias command, 34
    Open Image in New Window command, 127
    Open With command, 31
    Safari, 25
    Send File command, 149
    Show in Finder command, 35
    Show Original command, 35
contrast, increase, 17
conversion
    of audio files, 80, 97
    of image files, 57
copies of files and folders
    images from Web site, 126
    make, 32–33
Copy command (Edit menu)
    Finder, 36
    iMovie, 85
Copy *"Filename"* command, 33
Copy Image to Clipboard command, 126
CPU or processor
    Activity Monitor, 105
    System Profiler information, 104
cropping sound or music files, 96–97
CRT monitors, font smoothing and, 9
Customize Toolbar command (Finder View menu), 44

D

data CDs, burn with iTunes, 82
Date & Time pane (System Preferences), 10–11
defragmenting hard drives, 102
deletion or removal
    of color from display (grayscale), 17
    of dock icons, 42
    empty Trash securely, 63
    of Finder toolbar buttons, 19, 44
    of handle in iMovie, 63
    of Places sidebar items, 22–23
    of process by Activity Monitor, 105
    of Startup items, 65
    uninstall applications, 109
desktop. *See also* **Finder**
    alert sound, 12–13
    background
        add your own, 4–5
        change automatically, 6
        Fill Screen versus Tile option, 5
        focus aided by change to, 2
    change video resolution, 8
    clock configuration, 10–11
    font smoothing, 9
    menu bar
        change video resolution from, 8
        clock, 10
        volume control, 12–13
    productivity and, 2
    rebuild Classic mode, 112–113
    Stickies, 61
    visual and audio aids, 16–17
    White on Black text option, 7, 16–17
Desktop & Screen Saver pane (System Preferences)
    add desktop background, 4–5
    change desktop automatically, 6
    Change picture check box, 6
    Fill Screen option, 5
    Pictures folder shortcut, 5
    Tile option, 5
desktop publishing, mouse tracking speed for, 14
diagnostic programs. *See also* **troubleshooting**
    Activity Monitor, 105
    Disk Utility, 102–103
    System Profiler, 104
dictionary, find words in, 129
digital camera, 78, 79
Digital clock configuration, 10–11
Digital Hub, 76
directories. *See* **folders**
Disk Utility, 102–103
DiskWarrior (Alsoft), 108
display (screen). *See also* **colors**
    capture screenshots, 71
    change video resolution, 8
    font smoothing, 9
    grayscale, 17
    increase contrast, 17
    White on Black text option, 7, 16–17
    Zoom feature, 16–17

INDEX

displaying. *See* **viewing**
Displays pane (System Preferences), 8
dock
add folders, 42
add icons, 42
add Web sites, 43
aliaslike functionality, 35
delete icons, 42
hide automatically, 45
keyboard shortcuts, 26
overview, 42
relocate, 45
resize icons, 45
Show in Finder option, 35
toggle between applications, 26
Dock pane (System Preferences), 45
double-click speed for mouse, 14
downloading. *See also* **Internet resources**
files with FTP, 138–139
images from Internet, 126
drop-down list box colors, 7
Duplicate command, 32
DV format for QuickTime movies, 92
DVD drives
burn DVDs with iDVD, 81
burn DVDs with iTunes, 82–83
choose action for DVDs, 54
in Finder Places sidebar, 18, 22
format discs, 54
hide icons on desktop, 15
DVD Player, 54

E

echo effects in movies, 85
Edit menu
Copy command
Finder, 36
iMovie, 85
Paste command
Finder, 33, 36
iMovie, 85
Speech command (TextEdit), 75
e-mail. *See* **Mail application**
Empty Trash command (Finder menu), 63
encryption (FileVault), 38–39, 64
Energy Saver pane (System Preferences), 50
Entourage (Microsoft), 73
erasure. *See* **deletion or removal**
events (iCal), 72–73
Export command (File menu)
Finder, 57
iMovie, 92
Export dialog box (iMovie), 92–93
Export Photos dialog box (iPhoto), 94–95
Export Vcard menu item, 131
Exposé, 40, 46
Exposé pane (System Preferences), 46

F

fades (audio) in iMovie, 88–89
fast-user-switching feature, 49
Fax dialog box, 151
File menu
Color Label command (Finder), 29
Duplicate command (Finder), 32
Export command
Finder, 57
iMovie, 92
Get Info command
Finder, 30, 36
iTunes, 96
Make Alias command (Finder), 34
New from Pasteboard command (Preview), 127
Open command
Finder, 37
TextEdit, 74
Print command
any application, 151
Finder, 67
System Profiler, 104
Save As command (Safari), 127
Save command (Finder), 37
file transfer with iChat, 148–149
files. *See also* **folders**
alias creation, 35–36
choose application to open, 31
compression formats, 149
convert audio, 80
copy, 32–33
customize icons, 36
drag to copy or move, 32, 33
FileVault encryption, 38–39, 64
find, 28
in Finder Places sidebar, 22–23
Get Info window, 30
labels, 29
Mac file structure, 118
move to spring-loaded folders, 24
open, 31, 37
permissions, 30
restore from Trash, 63
save, 37
Save As PDF feature, 58, 67, 119
share with iChat, 148–149
target for alias, 35
verify structure of drive, 103
Windows file sharing, 143
FileVault encryption, 38–39, 64
Fill Screen option for background image, 5
Finder, 18
add font to Font Book, 70
contextual menus, 25
customize, 18–19
drag files to copy or move, 32, 33
drag image from Web site to, 127
find files, 28
go to parent folder, 52
importance, 18, 20

keyboard shortcuts, 26
labels, 29
Mac OS X Panther improvements, 20, 22
minimize window, 51
Places sidebar
   add items, 23
   open Preview from, 56
   overview, 18, 22
   remove items, 22–23
   show or hide, 23, 51
   using, 22–23
Search field, 28
share music on network drive, 136–137
show alias in, 35
sort files, 29
spring-loaded folders, 24
toolbar
   add or remove buttons, 19, 44
   display text labels only, 44
   move divider bar, 19
   show or hide, 18, 51
   use small icons, 44
   View buttons, 18
toolbar button, 51
Undo function, 33
views, 18–19
Finder menu
current username, 49
Empty Trash command, 63
Help command, 101
Secure Empty Trash command, 63
Finder Preferences dialog box
Connected Servers option, 138
show or hide desktop icons, 15
spring-loaded folder preferences, 24
finding. *See also* Sherlock application
application files, 109
files, 28
movies on Internet, 128
services with Rendezvous, 125
target file or folder for alias, 35
text in PDF files, 57
words in dictionary, 129
firewall, 142
FireWire, 60, 104
Flash Screen effect for alert sound, 16–17
folders. *See also* files
add to dock, 42
alias creation, 35–36
for applications, 109
change directories in UNIX, 62
copy, 32–33
customize icons, 36
display contents in UNIX, 42
drag to copy or move, 32, 33
FileVault encryption, 38–39, 64
find target for alias, 35
in Finder Places sidebar, 22–23
for FTP server, 139
Get Info window, 30
on Go menu, 52
go to parent folder, 52
labels, 29

permissions, 30
spring-loaded, 24
System folder for Classic mode launch, 113
Font Book utility, 70
font smoothing, 9
fonts, add, 70
Force Quit Applications dialog box, 100
Force Quit command ( menu), 100
frozen applications, force to quit, 100, 146–147
FTP, download files with, 138–139

G

games, mouse tracking speed for, 14
Get Info command (File menu)
Finder, 30, 36
iTunes, 96
GIF images, 56–57. *See also* images
Go menu, using, 52
Go to My Card command (Address Book Card menu), 69
Grab utility, 71
graphics. *See* images

H

hard drives
Activity Monitor, 105
boot drive problems, 103
defragment, 102
Disk Utility for errors, 102–103
in Finder Places sidebar, 18, 22
hide icons on desktop, 15
mount shared drive, 136–137
share music on network, 134, 136–137
Startup Disk pane and external drives, 68
hardware. *See also* specific kinds
printer sharing, 144–145
System Profiler information, 104
Help. *See also* technical support; troubleshooting
AppleCare Knowledge Base, 106
Mac OS X online Help system, 101
for UNIX commands, 62
Help command (Finder menu), 101
hiding. *See* viewing, show or hide
Highlight color, 7
Home folder
activate FileVault, 38, 64
deactivate FileVault, 39
on Go menu, 52
icon with FileVault active, 38
multiple users and, 110
hung applications, force to quit, 100, 146–147

I

iCal, 72–73
iChat
AOL Instant Messenger compatibility, 135
audio and video conferencing, 135
customize background, 150
keyboard shortcuts, 150
share files with, 148–149

INDEX

Icon view (Finder), 18–19
icons
    add to dock, 42
    aliases, 34–35
    customize for files and folders, 26
    delete from dock, 42
    display or hide on desktop, 15
    Home directory with FileVault active, 39
    resize dock icons, 45
    show or hide on desktop, 15
iDisk on Go menu, 52
iDVD, 81, 93
images. *See also* iDVD; iMovie; iPhoto
    change for user account, 111
    convert format, 57
    copy from Web site, 126
    create new from Clipboard copy, 127
    desktop background, 2, 4–6
    display information in Preview, 57
    download, 126
    erase after transfer from digital camera, 78–79
    export from iPhoto, 94–95
    from iPhoto in iMovie, 86–87
    Ken Burns Effect, 90–91
    launch iPhoto for picture CDs, 54
    for My Card (Address Book), 69
    save from Internet, 126–127
    screenshots, 71
    size ratio for iMovie, 87
    transfer from digital camera, 78
    view in Safari, 118
    view with Preview, 56–57
iMovie
    capture video from camera, 78
    delete handle, 89
    echo effects, 85
    export to camera, 92
    export to iDVD, 93
    fade audio in and out, 88–89
    iPhoto images in, 86–87
    iTunes audio in, 84–85
    Ken Burns Effect, 90–91
    overview, 84, 86
    QuickTime formats, 93
    recover deleted handle, 89
    size ratio for images, 87
    Undo function, 89
information
    Activity Monitor, 105
    AppleCare Knowledge Base, 106
    for files or folders, 30
    find with Sherlock, 128–129
    for images in Preview, 57
    iPod SysInfo text, 153
    System Profiler, 104
    for user accounts, 110
installing
    Apache Web server setup, 123
    Sherlock plug-ins, 129
    uninstall applications, 109

Internet resources. *See also* Mail application; Safari Web
    browser; Sherlock application; Web pages
    Acrobat Reader, 67
    Aladdin Systems Spring Cleaning, 109
    DiskWarrior (Alsoft), 108
    download files with FTP, 138–139
    download images, 126–127
    find movies, 128
    hard drive defragmenting utilities, 102
    look up words in dictionary, 129
    Mac OS X Panther improvements, 114
    Norton Utilities, 108
    save content, 126–127
    update Mac OS X, 107
    update time, 11
iPhoto
    create slideshow in iDVD, 81
    edit images, 86
    export album as Web pages, 94–95
    export images as QuickTime slideshow, 95
    export images from albums, 95
    export JPG images, 94
    Ken Burns Effect, 90–91
    launch for picture CDs, 54
    transfer photos from digital camera, 78
    use images in iMovie, 86–87
iPod
    iCal with iSync and, 72
    iSync with, 60
    share music over network, 152–153
    view hidden files with Terminal, 152, 153
    view SysInfo text, 153
iSync, 60, 72
iTunes
    activate sharing, 134
    burn CDs and DVDs, 82–83
    burn multiple identical discs, 83
    convert audio files, 80, 97
    create playlists, 83
    crop and split files, 96–97
    get music, 79
    launch for audio CDs, 54
    overview, 82
    preferences
        Burning options, 82
        Importing options, 80, 97
        Sharing options, 134
    share music on network drive, 136–137
    share music over network, 134
    use audio in iMovie, 84–85

J

Jobs, Steve (Apple executive), 76
JPG images. *See also* images
    convert TIFF images to, 57
    for desktop background, 5
    export from iPhoto, 94
    PNG images versus, 94
    TIFF images versus, 94
    view with Preview, 56–57
jukebox, iTunes sharing as, 134

K

Ken Burns Effect, 90–91
Keyboard & Mouse pane (System Preferences)
  keyboard shortcut options, 26–27, 53
  mouse settings, 14
keyboard shortcuts
  add, 53
  alias creation, 34
  change configuration for view mode, 19
  change global shortcuts, 53
  copy files, 32–33
  create, 26
  empty Trash, 63
  Exposé, 46
  Find window, 28
  iChat, 150
  modifier keys, 26
  open System Preferences panes, 26
  options, 27
  overview, 26–27
  Preview, 57
  restart Mac, 48
  right-click mechanism of mouse, 25
  Safari, 116–117
  show or hide Finder toolbar, 51
  shut down Mac, 48
  Shutdown window, 27
  sleep mode, 48
  spring-loaded folders, 24
  Stickies, 61
  toggle dock applications, 26
  Undo function, 33
  White on Black text option, 17
  Zoom feature, 16, 17
kill pidnumber command (UNIX), 147
Knowledge Base (AppleCare), 106

L

labels, 29
laptops with iCal and iSync, 72
launching or running. See also booting
  Activity Monitor, 105
  applications for CDs and DVDs, 54
  Disk Utility, 102
  FTP server, 138–139
  multiple Mac OS versions, 68
  recent items, 47
  Startup items, 50, 65
  System Profiler, 104
  Terminal application (UNIX), 62, 141
LCD displays, font smoothing and, 9
Levine, John R. (UNIX For Dummies), 62
List view, 18–19, 37
locked-up applications, force to quit, 100, 146–147
login
  automatic, for single-user system, 111
  desktop image change triggered by, 6
  remote, 140–141, 147
  turn on speakable items at, 66

LP records, crop and split files from, 96–97
ls command (UNIX), 62, 153

M

Mac Help Viewer window, 101
Mac OS
  run multiple versions, 68
  System folder for Classic mode launch, 113
  update Mac OS X, 107
Mac OS X services, 55
.Mac service, 72
Mail application
  Address Book with, 130–131
  attach Vcard to e-mail, 131
  export addresses, 131
  Mac OS X Panther improvements, 114
  preferences, 121
  stop spam, 121
  threaded e-mail, 122
Make Alias command, 34
man command (UNIX), 62, 140
manuals, bookmark in Safari, 118
master password, 38, 64
memory
  Activity Monitor, 105
  System Profiler information, 104
menus. See also specific menus
  add keyboard shortcut, 53
  change colors, 7
  contextual
    access commands, 25
    Color Label command, 29
    Copy "Filename" command, 33
    Copy Image to Clipboard command, 126
    Duplicate command, 32
    Finder, 25
    Make Alias command, 34
    Open Image in New Window command, 127
    Open With command, 31
    Safari, 25
    Send File command, 149
    Show in Finder command, 35
    Show Original command, 35
  desktop menu bar, 8, 10, 12–13
  Go menu, 52
  keyboard shortcuts, 26
  Services menu, 55
Micromat hard drive defragmenter, 102
microphone for iChat, 135
Microsoft
  Entourage, 73
  Windows computers
    file sharing with, 143
    printer sharing with, 144–145
  Word versus TextEdit, 74
mobile phones. See cellphones
monitor. See display (screen)
mouse
  corners for Exposé commands, 46
  double-click speed, 14

INDEX

mouse *(continued)*
  drag items
    add or remove dock icons, 42
    bookmarks, 124
    copy files or folders, 32, 33
    create aliases, 35
    editing text in TextEdit, 75
    Finder toolbar buttons, 19, 44
    Finder toolbar divider bar, 19
    font to Font Book, 70
    image from Web site to Finder, 127
    move files between drives, 32
    music files from network drive, 137
    name from Address Book, 131
    photos in iMovie, 87
    on Places sidebar, 22–23
    share files with iChat, 148
    songs to playlist in iTunes, 83
    sounds in iMovie, 84–85
    to spring-loaded folders, 24
    Web sites to dock, 43
  right-click mechanism, 25
  tracking speed, 14
MOV format for QuickTime movies, 92
movies. *See also* **iDVD; iMovie**
  capture from video camera, 78
  echo effects in, 85
  find on Internet, 128
  launch DVD Player for, 54
  QuickTime
    export iPhoto images as slideshow, 94–95
    preset formats in iMovie, 92–93
    save in Safari, 127
MP3 format, 80, 82
multimedia chat with iChat, 135
multiple Mac OS installations, 68, 113
music. *See also* **audio CDs; iTunes; sounds**
  burn CDs with iTunes, 82–83
  crop and split files, 96–97
  fade in and out in iMovie, 88–89
  import audio CD tracks to iTunes, 78–79
  iTunes audio in iMovie, 84–85
  share on network drive, 136–137
  share over network with iPod, 152–153
  share over network with iTunes, 134
  view iPod files with Terminal, 152, 153
mute sounds, 12–13
My Card (Address Book), 69

network. *See also* **servers**
  Activity Monitor, 105
  audio and video conferencing, 135
  burn CD using files over, 137
  drives in Finder Places sidebar, 22
  firewall, 142
  force program to quit, 146–147
  hide desktop icons for servers, 15
  Mac OS X Panther improvements, 132
  overview, 132
  printer sharing, 144–145
  remotely control other computers, 140–141, 146–147

  Rendezvous technology, 125
  servers on Go menu, 52
  share files with iChat, 148–149
  share iPod music over, 152–153
  share music on drive, 136–137
  share music with iTunes, 134
  surf local Web sites, 125
  System Profiler information for, 104
  Web server setup, 123
  Windows file sharing, 143
New from Pasteboard command (Preview File menu), 127
Norton SystemWorks application, 63
Norton Utilities, 102, 108
notes
  for iCal events, 73
  Stickies, 61

O

Open command (File menu)
  Finder, 37
  TextEdit, 74
Open dialog box, 37, 75
Open Image in New Window command, 127
Open With command, 31
opening. *See* **launching or running**
operating systems, switch, 68
orientation for PDF document, 67

P

Page Setup dialog box, 67
parent folder, go to, 52
passwords
  change for user account, 110
  FileVault encryption and, 64
  set master, 38
Paste command (Edit menu)
  Finder, 33, 36
  iMovie, 85
PDAs, 60, 72
PDF (Portable Document Format) files
  Save As PDF feature, 58, 67
  save Web pages as, 119
  search in Preview, 57
  view with Preview, 56–57
performance. *See also* **speed**
  font smoothing and, 9
  monitor for Mac, 105
permissions, 30, 103. *See also* **privileges**
photos. *See* **images**
Photoshop (Adobe), 87
PICT images, 56–57. *See also* **images**
pictures. *See* **images**
Pictures folder, 5
Places sidebar (Finder)
  add items, 23
  open Preview from, 56
  overview, 18, 22
  remove items, 22–23
  show or hide, 23, 51
  using, 22–23
Places sidebar (Open dialog box), 37

Places sidebar (Save dialog box), 37
playlists (iTunes)
    create, 83
    customize, 134
    share on network drive, 136–137
    share over network with iTunes, 134
plug-ins for Sherlock, 129
PNG images, 56–57, 94. *See also* **images**
pop-up ads, 120
portable devices, iSync with, 60
ports, deactivate, 142
power failure, automatic start up after, 50
Power key, 27
preferences
    Finder Preferences dialog box, 15, 24, 138
    iTunes, 80, 82, 97, 134
    Mail, 121
    Safari, 116
    System Preferences dialog box
        Accounts pane, 49, 65
        Appearance pane, 7, 9
        CDs & DVDs pane, 54
        Classic pane, 112–113
        Date & Time pane, 10–11
        Desktop & Screen Saver pane, 4–6
        Displays pane, 8, 26
        Dock pane, 45
        Keyboard & Mouse pane, 14, 26–27, 53
        Security pane, 38–39, 64
        Sharing pane, 123, 139, 140, 142, 143, 144, 147, 152
        Software Update pane, 107
        Sound pane, 12–13, 26
        Speech pane, 66
        Startup Disk pane, 68
        Universal Access pane, 7, 16–17
    TextEdit, 75
Preview, 56–57, 119
Print command (File menu)
    any application, 151
    Finder, 67
    System Profiler, 104
Print dialog box
    Fax pane, 151
    Save As PDF feature, 67
    for shared printer, 145
printer sharing, 144–145
privileges, 111. *See also* **permissions**
processes, 105
processor. *See* **CPU or processor**
programs. *See* **applications**

Q

QuickTime movies
    export iPhoto images as slideshow, 94–95
    preset formats in iMovie, 92–93
    save in Safari, 127
QuickTime Pro, 93
quitting
    force program to quit, 100, 146–147
    shut down Mac, 27, 48, 50
    Terminal application (UNIX), 62

R

read permissions. *See* **permissions**
Recent Items list, 47
remote control for other computers, 140–141, 146–147
removable drives. *See* *specific kinds*
removal. *See* **deletion or removal**
Rendezvous technology, 125
resolution, video, 2, 8
Restart command (menu), 108
right-click mechanism of mouse, 25
Roxio Toast, 92
RTF (Rich Text Formatting) files, 74
running. *See* **launching or running**

S

Safari menu
    Block Pop-Up Windows command, 120
    Preferences command, 116
Safari Preferences window, 116
Safari Web browser. *See also* **Internet resources**
    add Web sites to dock, 43
    bookmarks, 118
    close all tabs, 117
    contextual menus, 25
    as document viewer, 118
    download files with FTP, 138–139
    enable tabs, 116
    keyboard shortcuts, 116–117
    Mac OS X Panther improvements, 114
    open image file, 118
    preferences, 116
    save Web pages as PDF files, 119
    stop pop-up ads, 120
    surf local Web sites, 125
    surf sites for people in Address Book, 124
    using tabs, 116–117
Samba technology, 143
Save As command (Safari File menu), 127
Save As PDF feature
    usefulness, 58
    using, 67
    for Web pages, 119
Save command (Finder File menu), 37
Save dialog box, 37, 71
Save to File dialog box, 67
saving
    files, 37
    Internet content, 126–127
    as PDF, 58, 67, 119
    QuickTime movies in Safari, 127
    Web pages, 119
scale of PDF document, 67
screen. *See* **display (screen)**
Screen Grab dialog box, 71
screenshots, 71
searching. *See* **finding**
Secure Empty Trash command (Finder menu), 63
security. *See also* **passwords; permissions; privileges**
    deactivate ports, 142
    FileVault encryption, 38–39, 64
    firewall, 142

INDEX

security *(continued)*
    remote login and, 141
    Secure Empty Trash option, 63
    set master password, 38
Security pane (System Preferences), 38–39, 64
Send File command, 149
servers
    FTP, 138–139
    on Go menu, 52
    hide desktop icons, 15
    music, 134, 136–137
    Web server setup, 123
    for Windows file sharing, 143
services
    find with Rendezvous, 125
    using, 55
Services menu, 55
Set Chat Background command (iChat View menu), 150
sharing. *See* network; servers
Sharing pane (System Preferences)
    Apache Web server setup, 123
    firewall activation, 142
    FTP Access option, 139
    Personal File Sharing option, 152
    Printer Sharing option, 144
    Remote Login option, 140, 147
    Windows file sharing activation, 143
Sherlock application
    AppleCare and, 106
    find information, 128–129
    as Internet tool, 28
    move plug-in icon in toolbar, 129
    overview, 128
    plug-ins, 129
Show in Finder command, 35
Show Original command, 35
showing. *See* viewing, show or hide
Sleep command (⌘ menu), 48
sleep mode, 6, 48
smiley faces in iChat, 150
software. *See* applications
Software Update pane (System Preferences), 107
songs. *See* music
Sound pane (System Preferences), 12–13, 26
sounds. *See also* iTunes; music
    alert, 12–13
    crop and split files, 96–97
    echo effects in movies, 85
    fade in and out in iMovie, 88–89
    iTunes audio in iMovie, 84–85
    mute, 12–13
    speak text in TextEdit, 75
    user interface sound effects, 13
    voice commands, 66
    volume control, 12–13
    volume key sound effects, 13
spam, 121
Speech command (TextEdit Edit menu), 75
Speech pane (System Preferences), 66
speed
    mouse settings, 14
    performance, 9, 105

spell checker, disable in TextEdit, 75
splitting sound or music files, 96–97
spoken commands, 66
Spring Cleaning (Aladdin Systems), 109
spring-loaded folders, 24
ssh (remote control) program, 140–141, 146–147
startup. *See* launching or running
Startup Disk pane (System Preferences), 68
Startup items, 50, 65
Stickies, 61
stopping. *See also* quitting
    pop-up ads, 120
    spam, 121
SysInfo text (iPod), 153
system boot menu, 108
System folder for Classic mode launch, 113
System Preferences dialog box
    Accounts pane, 49, 65
    Appearance pane, 7, 9
    CDs & DVDs pane, 54
    Classic pane, 112–113
    Date & Time pane, 10–11
    Desktop & Screen Saver pane, 4–6
    Displays pane, 8, 26
    Dock pane, 45
    Energy Saver pane, 50
    Exposé pane, 46
    Keyboard & Mouse pane, 14, 26–27, 53
    keyboard shortcuts, 26
    Security pane, 38–39, 64
    Sharing pane
        Apache Web server setup, 123
        firewall activation, 142
        FTP Access option, 139
        Personal File Sharing option, 152
        Printer Sharing option, 144
        Remote Login option, 140, 147
        Windows file sharing activation, 143
    Software Update pane, 107
    Sound pane, 12–13, 26
    Speech pane, 66
    Startup Disk pane, 68
    Universal Access pane, 7, 16–17
System Profiler, 104

T

tabbed browsing, 116–117
target file or folder for alias, 35
technical support. *See also* Help; troubleshooting
    AppleCare Knowledge Base, 106
    System Profiler information for, 104
Terminal application (UNIX). *See also* UNIX
    launch, 62, 141
    quit, 62
    remotely control other computers, 140–141, 146–147
    view iPod music files, 152, 153
terminating. *See* closing; quitting
text
    edit files with TextEdit, 74–75
    font smoothing, 9
    speak in TextEdit, 75

TextEdit, 74–75, 153
threaded e-mail, 122
TIFF images. *See also* images
    convert to JPG format, 57
    for desktop background, 5
    export from iPhoto, 94
    JPG images versus, 94
    screenshots, 71
    view with Preview, 56–57
Tile option for background image, 5
time
    announcement feature, 10
    automatic startup and shutdown, 50
    clock configuration, 10–11
    international format, 10
    spring-loaded folder delay, 24
    update over the Internet, 11
To Do items, share with portable devices, 72
Toast (Roxio), 92
toolbar (Finder)
    add or remove buttons, 19, 44
    display text labels only, 44
    move divider bar, 19
    show or hide, 18, 51
    use small icons, 44
    View buttons, 18
Tracking Speed option for mouse, 14
Trash, 63
troubleshooting. *See also* technical support
    AppleCare Knowledge Base for, 106
    boot from CD-ROM, 103, 108
    delete a process, 105
    force program to quit, 100, 146–147
    get information with System Profiler, 104
    hard drives with Disk Utility, 102–103
    monitor performance, 105
    online Help system for, 101
    overview, 98
    rebuild Classic mode desktop, 112–113
    uninstall applications, 109
    update Mac OS X, 107
    user account problems, 110–111
24-hour clock display, 11

U

Undo function
    Finder, 33
    iMovie, 89
uninstalling applications, 109
Universal Access pane (System Preferences), 7, 16–17
UNIX
    age of, 139
    applications included with Mac OS X Panther, 62
    change directories, 62
    display directory contents, 42
    launch Terminal application, 62, 141
    quit Terminal application, 62
    ssh (remote control) program, 140–141, 146–147
UNIX For Dummies (Levine, John R. and Young, Margaret Levine), 62
updating
    Mac OS X, 107
    time over the Internet, 11

URLs. *See* Internet resources
USB, 60, 104
User Switch menu, 49
users
    Admin account, 111
    automatic login, 111
    change image, 111
    change password, 110
    change privileges, 111
    switch between, 49
    view account information, 110
    Web sites created by Apache, 123, 125

V

vCal data files, import in iCal, 73
Vcard, export from Address Book, 131
video camera
    export iMovies to, 92
    get video from, 78
    for iChat, 135
video conferencing with iChat, 135
video resolution, 2, 8
View menu
    Clear Background command (iChat), 150
    Customize Toolbar command (Finder), 44
    Set Chat Background command (iChat), 150
viewing. *See also* display (screen)
    documents in Safari, 118
    file or folder information, 30
    image information in Preview, 57
    images in Preview, 56–57
    iPod files with Terminal, 152, 153
    PDF files in Preview, 119
    permissions, 30
    show or hide
        Classic launch progress bar, 112
        desktop icons, 15
        Finder toolbar, 18, 51
        Places sidebar, 23, 51
    SysInfo text on iPod, 153
    threaded e-mail, 122
    Zoom feature for, 16–17
views
    change configuration for all windows, 19
    Finder, 18–19, 22
    Open dialog box, 37
    Save dialog box, 37
visual aids, 7, 16–17
voice commands, 66
volume control, 12–13

W-X

WAV format, convert files to, 80
Web browser. *See* Safari Web browser
Web pages. *See also* Internet resources; Safari Web browser; Sherlock application
    add to dock, 43
    default creation by Apache, 123, 125
    export albums from iPhoto as, 94–95
    personal, 123
    save as PDF, 119

INDEX

Web pages *(continued)*
    save content, 126–127
    Web server setup, 123
Web server setup, 123
White on Black text option, 7, 16–17
windows. *See also specific windows*
    capture screenshots, 71
    change view mode configuration, 19
    Finder, 22
    Search field, 28
    Stickies, 61
    switch with Exposé, 46
Windows (Microsoft) computers
    file sharing with, 143
    printer sharing with, 144–145
Word (Microsoft) versus TextEdit, 74
write permissions. *See* **permissions**

Y-Z

Young, Margaret Levine (*UNIX For Dummies*), 62

Zip drives, hide icons on desktop, 15
Zoom feature, 16–17

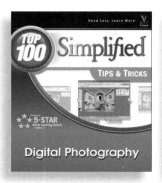
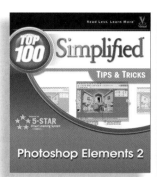
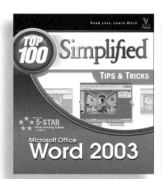

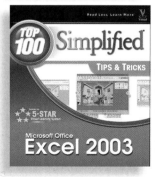

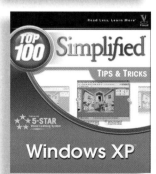
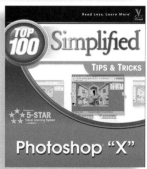

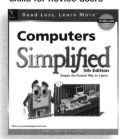